ILLINOIS TEST PREP
IAR Practice Test Book
English Language Arts
Grade 5

© 2019 by L. Hawas

All rights reserved. No part of this book may be reproduced or transmitted in any form or by any means, electronic, mechanical, photocopying, recording, or otherwise without prior written permission.

ISBN 978-1795160049

TEST MASTER PRESS

www.testmasterpress.com

IAR Practice Test Book, English Language Arts, Grade 5

CONTENTS

Introduction	4
Practice for the IAR English Language Arts Tests	5
Set 1: Literary Texts with Writing Task	5
Set 2: Informational Texts with Writing Task	23
Set 3: Literary Text with Narrative Writing Task	41
Set 4: Short Informational Text	50
Set 5: Short Literary Text	58
Set 6: Long Informational Text	66
Set 7: Paired Literary Passages	76
Set 8: Literary Texts with Writing Task	89
Set 9: Informational Texts with Writing Task	106
Set 10: Literary Text with Narrative Writing Task	122
Set 11: Short Informational Text	131
Set 12: Short Literary Text	141
Set 13: Long Informational Text	149
Set 14: Paired Informational Passages	160
Answer Key	**173**
Set 1: Literary Texts with Writing Task	174
Set 2: Informational Texts with Writing Task	176
Set 3: Literary Text with Narrative Writing Task	178
Set 4: Short Informational Text	180
Set 5: Short Literary Text	181
Set 6: Long Informational Text	182
Set 7: Paired Literary Passages	183
Set 8: Literary Texts with Writing Task	185
Set 9: Informational Texts with Writing Task	187
Set 10: Literary Text with Narrative Writing Task	189
Set 11: Short Informational Text	191
Set 12: Short Literary Text	192
Set 13: Long Informational Text	194
Set 14: Paired Informational Passages	196

INTRODUCTION
For Parents, Teachers, and Tutors

About the New Illinois Assessment of Readiness

In 2019, students in Illinois will take a new test instead of the previously used PARCC assessments. The new test is the Illinois Assessment of Readiness, or IAR. This practice test book will prepare students for the IAR tests.

Key Features of the New Illinois Assessment of Readiness

The key features of the IAR tests are described below.

- The tests cover the skills listed in the Illinois Learning Standards.
- The tests have a greater emphasis on writing skills. Students will have to provide more written answers, as well as write essays and narratives.
- The tests include paired questions. A first question will ask about a text, and a second question will expand on the first, often by asking for evidence.
- The tests include technology-enhanced questions. These may involve tasks like placing items in order, highlighting sentences from a text, or completing webs and diagrams.
- The tests focus on close reading and using evidence from the texts. Questions will require students to read texts closely and to use specific evidence from the text.

This book has been specifically designed to prepare students for these key features. The practice sets include all the types of questions that students will find on the real IAR tests.

Types of Tasks on the New Illinois Assessment of Readiness

The new IAR tests are made up of 2 units, with each unit taking 90 minutes to complete. The types of tasks that may be found on the test are summarized below.

- A set of two literary texts with individual questions and an essay question on both
- A set of three informational texts with individual questions and an essay question on all
- A literary text with a narrative writing task based on the passage
- Short and long literary texts with a range of question types
- Short and long informational texts with a range of question types
- Paired literary or informational texts with a range of question types

The practice sets in this book will prepare students for the tasks they need to complete on the real IAR tests. There are sets for all the types of tasks found on the real tests. The questions within each set are similar to what students will find on the real IAR tests, except that each set contains more questions than the real test. This will ensure that students experience all the types of questions they are likely to encounter on the real test.

IAR Practice Test Book, English Language Arts, Grade 5

IAR Practice

Set 1

Literary Texts with Writing Task

Instructions

This set has two passages for you to read. Read each passage and answer the questions that follow it.

For each multiple-choice question, fill in the circle for the correct answer. For other types of questions, follow the instructions given. Some of the questions require a written answer. Write your answer on the lines provided.

After reading both passages, you will answer an essay question. You will use information from both passages to answer this question. Write your answer on the lines provided.

The Lighthouse

Simon was fascinated with the lighthouse to the south of the island. It was just two miles from his front door. The lighthouse stood proudly above the sea and cast its light for miles. It had stood in that spot for over two hundred years. Wind and rain had battered it, but the lighthouse stood strong and sturdy. During the day, you could see the aging of the old stone bricks.

Simon often stared at the lighthouse and wondered about its history. He had even heard rumors that it was haunted by a stonemason that had helped build it. He had been told the stonemason's initials were carved into some of the stones. Simon had never been close enough to see it for himself. At night it was an eerie presence. The white stones shone in the moonlight like a ghost hovering over the sea. Simon knew the lighthouse was meant to protect sailors. But sometimes he felt like it was watching him. Simon and his friends were scared to even go near it.

One night, Rick was staying at Simon's house. Just like Simon, he couldn't help stare at the lighthouse.

"I think we should head over there," said Rick, who was Simon's best friend. He was always more adventurous than his sensible friend.

Simon thought carefully before responding.

"But aren't you scared?" he asked.

"Not at all. Are you?" Rick replied.

Simon did not want to look scared in front of his best friend.

"No," he replied nervously.

"That is settled then," said Rick. "We will head out this evening."

After dinner, they gathered some food and supplies and packed them into Rick's backpack. Then they headed out toward the lighthouse. Both boys were very quiet as they walked through the fields on the island.

"You're not saying much," said Simon. "Are you okay?"

"I'm fine," said Rick. "I was just thinking."

When they reached the shore, the sun was starting to set above the sea. The boys slowly climbed the small rock face as the sun went down. They both stopped as they stood in front of the lighthouse door.

"In you go then Simon," said Rick, gesturing toward the wooden door.

"You go first," said Simon. "It was your idea."

Rick paused and didn't say a single word. Then Rick edged toward the door. He stopped and looked back at Simon, who gave a small nod of encouragement. He arrived at the step and reached out for the door handle. Simon had stayed back in the shadows. As Rick twisted the handle, he suddenly heard a loud growling from inside.

"Run!" shouted Rick at the top of his voice.

He raced away, with Simon following close behind him. They ran back to the main road and headed back toward Simon's house. Rick looked very sheepish as they made their way home.

"Didn't you want to see inside?" asked Simon.

Rick shrugged and looked down at the ground.

"I guess it was scarier than I thought," he whispered.

"Oh, I don't know," said Simon. "It wasn't that bad."

1   Read this sentence from the passage.

   At night it was an eerie presence.

   Circle **all** the words that have about the same meaning as <u>eerie</u>.

   (creepy)   amusing   (ghostly)   useful

   gigantic   (scary)   calming   welcoming

2   Select the **three** details given about the lighthouse that best explain why Simon finds it eerie. Tick **three** boxes to show your choices.

   ☐ Simon is fascinated by it.

   ☐ It is two miles from Simon's house.

   ☐ It stands proudly above the sea.

   ☐ It casts its light for miles.

   ☐ It is two hundred years old.

   ☒ It is made of white stones that seem to shine at night.

   ☒ There are rumors that it is haunted.

   ☐ Simon has never been near it.

   ☐ Its job is to protect sailors.

   ☒ Simon feels like it is watching him.

3 Read this sentence from the passage.

   Then Rick edged toward the door.

   The word edged shows that Rick moved –
   - Ⓐ swiftly
   - **Ⓑ** slowly
   - Ⓒ suddenly
   - Ⓓ smoothly

4 Based on your answer to Question 3, what does the way Rick moves show about how he feels? Use details from the passage in your answer.

I think now that rick is a the door he gets scared I could tell because rick stoped and looked back a Simon like he was scared and nervos to open the wooden door.

5   Which statement is most likely true about Rick?

   Ⓐ   He is not scared of anything.

   ⬤   He is not as fearless as he says he is.

   Ⓒ   He enjoys seeing how scared Simon is.

   Ⓓ   He only pretends to be frightened.

6   Which word in the sentence below shows that the author is using personification?

   The lighthouse stood proudly above the sea and cast its light for miles.

   ⬤   *proudly*

   Ⓑ   *above*

   Ⓒ   *light*

   Ⓓ   *miles*

7   Why does Rick tell Simon to run?

   Ⓐ   He sees a creature inside the lighthouse.

   ⬤   He hears a noise from inside the lighthouse.

   Ⓒ   He thinks they are going to get in trouble for being inside the lighthouse.

   Ⓓ   He realizes that the owner of the lighthouse is home.

8   At the start of the passage, Rick says that he is not scared of going to the lighthouse. Describe **two** details that suggest that Rick is more scared than he admits.

1: When Rick stopped at the dore he felt a lot more scard because he didn't know what was inside

2: Rick wanted simon to go first, bot if Rick really wasn't scared he would go in first with no problem

9   What is the point of view in the passage?

Ⓐ   First person

Ⓑ   Second person

Ⓒ   Third person limited

Ⓓ   Third person omniscient

10   According to the passage, how is Simon different from Rick?

Ⓐ   He is more sensible.

Ⓑ   He is more adventurous.

Ⓒ   He is more intelligent.

Ⓓ   He is more determined.

11 Read this sentence from the passage.

Rick shrugged and looked down at the ground.

The author uses this description to suggest that Rick feels —

Ⓐ angry

Ⓑ embarrassed

Ⓒ amused

Ⓓ terrified

12 Circle the word below that you think best describes Simon. Explain why you made that choice.

(**brave**)   cowardly

I think Simon is more brave because he was scard to go to the light, but he did it anyway just for Rick

13 In the first two paragraphs below, the author gives details about the lighthouse. Complete the table by listing **three** examples of factual details and **three** examples of Simon's personal opinions or feelings.

Simon was fascinated with the lighthouse to the south of the island. It was just two miles from his front door. The lighthouse stood proudly above the sea and cast its light for miles. It had stood in that spot for over two hundred years. Wind and rain had battered it, but the lighthouse stood strong and sturdy. During the day, you could see the aging of the old stone bricks.

Simon often stared at the lighthouse and wondered about its history. He had even heard rumors that it was haunted by a stonemason that had helped build it. He had been told the stonemason's initials were carved into some of the stones. Simon had never been close enough to see it for himself. At night it was an eerie presence. The white stones shone in the moonlight like a ghost hovering over the sea. Simon knew the lighthouse was meant to protect sailors. But sometimes he felt like it was watching him. Simon and his friends were scared to even go near it.

Factual Details	Simon's Opinions or Feelings
I was 200 years old	It was eerie
It was hanted (Romars)	Simon and friends were scrant to go near it
It lights cased on for miles and miles	It looked like a goast at night

Tara's Fear

Tara was scared of flying. She always had been ever since she was a little girl. It hadn't been a problem for her as a child though, as her parents never took a vacation overseas. Despite this, Tara's fear grew steadily the older she got. She hated the idea of being up in the air and in flight.

One year her family announced that they would take their vacation abroad. They were going to New Zealand. Her father had planned an adventure trip that included white water rafting, fly fishing, and trekking up an old volcano. Tara had just turned 13 years old. Everything her father described sounded like the kind of great adventure she had only read about in books. She was excited by the thought of it all, but she couldn't stop thinking about the long flight there. She longed to go, but she didn't know if she could cope with the flight there. She was so distraught that she finally claimed that she simply could not go. As she lay crying on her bed at the thought, her father walked into her room.

"I can't do it, Dad," she said sobbing. "I won't be able to fly."

Her father placed his hand gently on her shoulder.

"I know honey," he whispered. "It's really difficult for you. I know exactly how you feel."

Tara looked up at her father. "Do you really?" she asked.

"When I was your age, I had a phobia too," he replied. "I never thought I'd ever get over it."

Tara sat upright on the bed. She would never have guessed that her father could be scared of anything.

"What were you scared of Dad?" she asked.

Her father looked at her before replying.

"It seems silly now, but I used to be scared of spiders. Whenever I saw one I would scream and run in the other direction. When I was young, I didn't even like playing outside because of spiders and small insects. One year my mother told me that we were going camping. I immediately refused to go. The idea of sleeping under the stars with all of those bugs scared the life out of me!"

"What happened then, Dad?" asked Tara.

"Well my mother talked to me," he replied. "She explained that she understood why I was scared, but that it was something that she could help me to overcome. Then she told me that once I did get over my fear, I would be able to enjoy being outdoors much more. She made me realize that I couldn't let a spider stop me from ever enjoying being outdoors. I had to focus on all the fun I would be having, not on the one thing that scared me."

A small smile crept across Tara's face.

"So did you go in the end then, Dad?" she asked.

"You bet I did," he replied without hesitation. "It was a challenge, but I kept thinking about my mother's words. They inspired me to face my fears. I went camping with my family and had the time of my life. You'll have the time of your life on our trip. You can't let your fear of the plane stop you from having all those good times. You just close your eyes and imagine yourself in New Zealand and don't let your fear take the good times away from you."

Tara suddenly felt determined. She was going to stand up to her fear and not let it steal her trip from her.

"Thanks Dad," said Tara. "You'd better make sure you book me a seat on the plane because I'm coming whether my fear likes it or not."

14 What does the word distraught mean in the sentence below?

She was so distraught that she finally claimed that she simply could not go.

Ⓐ   Disbelieving

● Ⓑ   Distressed

Ⓒ   Uncertain

Ⓓ   Determined

15 In the sentence below, which word means about the same as steadily?

Despite this, Tara's fear grew steadily the older she got.

Ⓐ   Swiftly

Ⓑ   Weirdly

Ⓒ   Suddenly

● Ⓓ   Gradually

16 How does Tara feel when her father first says that he had a phobia?

Ⓐ   Alarmed

● Ⓑ   Surprised

Ⓒ   Excited

Ⓓ   Relieved

17 Based on the information in paragraph 2, explain why Tara has mixed feelings about the trip to New Zealand. Use details from the passage to explain your answer.

Tara was scared to fly on a plane because she had a phobia of flying, but she was really excited to go on the trip

18 Read this sentence spoken by the father.

> **The idea of sleeping under the stars with all of those bugs scared the life out of me!**

Which literary device does the father use to emphasize how fearful he felt?

Ⓐ   Imagery, using details to create an image or picture

Ⓑ   Hyperbole, using exaggeration to make a point

Ⓒ   Simile, comparing two items using the words "like" or "as"

Ⓓ   Symbolism, using an object to stand for something else

19 Which statement best describes how you can tell that the passage is realistic fiction?

- Ⓐ It has a theme that can be applied in real life.
- ●Ⓑ It describes events that could really happen.
- Ⓒ It has a modern setting.
- Ⓓ It has a main problem.

20 How do the father's past experiences help him know how to help his daughter? Use details from the passage to support your answer.

he helped her by telling her the he had a phobia too.

21 How are Tara and Tara's father similar?

- Ⓐ They have the same fear of flying.
- Ⓑ They have never flown before.
- ●Ⓒ They receive help to overcome a fear from a parent.
- Ⓓ They are thoughtful and understanding.

22 The main theme of the passage is about –

- Ⓐ admitting your fears
- Ⓑ letting other people help you
- 🅒 not letting your fears hold you back
- Ⓓ making the most of every opportunity

23 Complete the cause and effect diagram below to show how Tara and Tara's father are affected by their fears.

Cause	Effect
Tara's Fear flying	**What It Prevents Her Doing** Didn't want to go on the trip
Tara's Father's Fear Spiders	**What It Prevents Him Doing** Didn't want to go camping

24 At the end of the passage, Tara says that she is going on the plane whether her fear likes it or not. Explain what Tara means by this.

Tara really want to go on the trip so she's not just going to let her fear take away a fun trip

25 In the passage, Tara wants to do the things her father has planned for them in New Zealand. Explain how this helps her be braver.

It makes her braver because she really wants to do them, so she faces her fear and goes on the plan

26 You have read two passages that involve a character facing a fear. Write an essay that compares Simon and Tara and how they face a fear. In your answer, give your opinion on which character is the bravest.

- Explain what each character is afraid of.
- Describe how each character faces a fear.
- Give an opinion on which character is the bravest.
- Use details from both passages to support your answer.

END OF SET 1

IAR Practice

Set 2

Informational Texts with Writing Task

Instructions

This set has three passages for you to read. Read each passage and answer the questions that follow it.

For each multiple-choice question, fill in the circle for the correct answer. For other types of questions, follow the instructions given. Some of the questions require a written answer. Write your answer on the lines provided.

After reading the three passages, you will answer an essay question. You will use information from all three passages to answer this question. Write your answer on the lines provided.

Mark Zuckerberg

Mark Zuckerberg is a web site developer and computer programmer. He is also a businessperson. He is best known for creating the web site Facebook. Facebook is a web site that allows people to connect with friends and family. He is now the CEO and president of the company.

Zuckerberg founded the web site in 2004 with some of his Harvard University classmates. He has since overseen the development of the site. Facebook became the most visited online web site throughout 2010. This was also the year that Mark Zuckerberg was named as Person of the Year by *Time Magazine*.

Mark Zuckerberg was born in White Plains, New York in 1984. His early education was spent at Ardsley High School. This was followed by Phillips Exeter Academy. While at Phillips Exeter Academy, he won prizes for his work in science, mathematics, astronomy, and physics. His outdoor pursuits included fencing, and he was captain of the college fencing team. He is also multilingual and can speak French, Latin, Hebrew, and Ancient Greek.

Zuckerberg first showed an interest in computers during middle school. At this time, he started to write software programs. His father hired an experienced software developer, David Newman, to tutor his son. He was identified at this young age to be an amazing talent. This encouraged him to take a graduate course in software design while at high school. He continued to develop computer programs as he learned.

Zuckerberg's main interest was in software that helped people to interact and communicate. This passion inspired a program called ZuckNet. This allowed a small set of users to communicate by 'pinging' each other. It was like a basic version of today's instant messenger tools. Zuckerberg continued to experiment with different software programs. Then he enrolled at Harvard University. During this time, he focused on creating software that connected people through common interests. The inspiration for Facebook came from paper-based books at the university. The books were known as facebooks and showed students' names, photographs, and gave information about them.

Facebook was launched on February 4, 2004. At first it was only for Harvard University students. It soon spread to other major universities including Stanford, Columbia, Yale, and MIT. This was followed by a spread to most universities in the United States. In 2005, it was made available to high schools. This was followed by allowing people from large companies like Apple and Microsoft to join. In 2006, it was made available to anyone over the age of 13. The site has grown rapidly since then. In 2012, Facebook had over one billion users worldwide.

On May 18, 2012, Facebook took another major step in its history. It listed on the stock exchange. It was one of the biggest listings in history. On the day of its listing, Facebook had a total value of just over $100 billion. Mark Zuckerberg was given the honor of ringing the bell to open stock market trading on the day. He rang the bell from the Facebook campus in California surrounded by cheering staff.

The site continues to grow and change. As of January 2014, Zuckerberg remains as chairman and CEO of Facebook, and has an estimated total wealth of just over $25 billion. In 2010, he pledged to give at least half of his wealth to charity over his lifetime. His donations have included giving over $100 million to public schools in New Jersey, supporting various small Internet businesses, and giving almost $1 billion worth of Facebook shares to the Silicon Valley Community Foundation.

One other thing Mark Zuckerberg is known for is wearing hoodies. While a suit and tie is the expected choice for a business meeting, he appears at many wearing a hoodie and slide-on sandals. This kind of casual clothing is also usually his choice for presentations and other public events. Some have said that his style of dress shows his lack of seriousness. Others argue that he values what he does above what he looks like.

© Elaine Chan and Priscilla Chan, Wikimedia Commons

1. As it is used in the sentence, what does the word <u>common</u> mean?

   During this time, he focused on creating software that connected people through common interests.

   Ⓐ   Ordinary

   Ⓑ   Everyday

   Ⓒ   Shared

   Ⓓ   General

2. Read this sentence from the passage.

   He is also multilingual and can speak French, Latin, Hebrew, and Ancient Greek.

   What does the prefix in the word <u>multilingual</u> mean? Explain how the sentence helps show the meaning of the prefix.

   _____

   _____

   _____

   _____

   _____

3 Place the following groups in order from first to gain access to Facebook to last to gain access to Facebook. Write the numbers 1, 2, 3, and 4 on the lines to show the order.

___ Students of major universities

___ Employees of large companies

___ High school students

___ Harvard University students

4 Which paragraph has the main purpose of describing how Zuckerberg first developed his computer skills? Circle the paragraph you have selected.

Paragraph 1   Paragraph 2   Paragraph 3   Paragraph 4

Paragraph 5   Paragraph 6   Paragraph 7   Paragraph 8

5 Which sentence from the passage best shows that Facebook is successful?

Ⓐ *Facebook is a web site that allows people to connect with friends and family.*

Ⓑ *Facebook became the most visited online web site throughout 2010.*

Ⓒ *Facebook was launched on February 4, 2004.*

Ⓓ *This was followed by allowing people from large companies like Apple and Microsoft to join.*

6 Why did Mark Zuckerberg's father most likely hire a software developer to tutor his son?

- Ⓐ He was worried that Mark was making mistakes.
- Ⓑ He saw that Mark had a talent worth developing.
- Ⓒ He saw that Mark was struggling with his studies.
- Ⓓ He wanted Mark to develop useful programs.

7 This passage is most like –

- Ⓐ a biography
- Ⓑ an autobiography
- Ⓒ a short story
- Ⓓ a news article

8 In paragraph 3, the author describes how Zuckerberg won prizes for his work in several areas, was captain of the fencing team, and is multilingual. Explain why you think the author chose to include these details.

_____

_____

_____

_____

_____

9 The web below summarizes information from the passage.

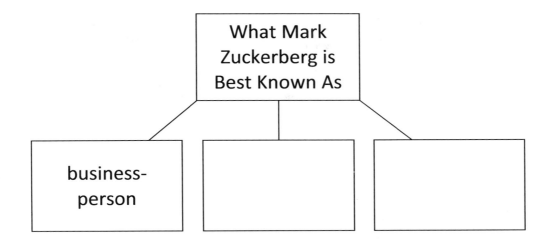

Complete the web by choosing the **two** best options from those given below. Write your answers in the web.

| teacher | fencing champion | computer programmer |

| web site developer | author | college professor |

10 The passage describes how successful Mark Zuckerberg has become. Describe **one** lesson about becoming successful people can learn from the passage. Use details from the passage in your answer.

_____

_____

_____

_____

_____

11 What does the photograph and the caption show about Zuckerberg's personality? Explain your answer.

_____

_____

_____

_____

_____

_____

Sir Isaac Newton

Sir Isaac Newton was an English-born physicist and mathematician. He also had a keen interest in astronomy, philosophy, alchemy, and theology. He was born on January 4, 1643 and died on March 31, 1727 at the age of 84. It was in the field of physics where Sir Isaac Newton carried out his best and most important work.

Newton is widely recognized as the first person to understand gravity. He also developed the three laws of motion. These laws became the foundations for scientists' work through the following centuries. Newton's work showed that the motion of objects is governed by a rigid set of natural laws. These laws applied to objects on the earth as well as the planets themselves.

Sir Isaac Newton's thirst for knowledge was applied to all aspects of science. He studied the speed of sound, and designed the first reflecting telescope for practical use. He also developed an advanced theory of color. He even developed a universal law of cooling.

Newton's Laws of Motion

Newton's First Law of Motion	An object will remain at rest unless acted on by an unbalanced force.
Newton's Second Law of Motion	The acceleration of an object depends on its mass and the net force.
Newton's Third Law of Motion	For every action, there is an equal and opposite reaction.

Sir Isaac Newton's work in the field of mathematics was also groundbreaking. His studies are said to have advanced every mathematics theory in practice today. Credit for some of his findings is shared with a German philosopher called Gottfried Leibniz. The basis of their work was applied to developing fractions and equations as mathematical tools. His continued hard work in the field led to him being appointed a Professor of Mathematics in 1669.

Sir Isaac Newton was also a deeply religious man. It is a little known fact that he wrote more papers on religion than he did on physics and mathematics. Many of his religious papers were ahead of their time. They were opposed to many beliefs held in the 17th century.

Sir Isaac Newton is widely considered to be one of the most influential men of all time. His work has inspired much of the scientific and mathematical knowledge that is widely used today. Despite this, Newton was a modest man who often praised the work of others who had gone before him. In 1999, a poll of modern experts revealed that Sir Isaac Newton was considered to be the greatest physicist of all time. He shared the title with Albert Einstein.

12 Read this sentence from the passage.

> **Despite this, Newton was a modest man who often praised the work of others who had gone before him.**

As it is used in the sentence, what does the word <u>modest</u> mean?

- Ⓐ Humble
- Ⓑ Kind
- Ⓒ Simple
- Ⓓ Shy

13 Read this sentence from the passage.

> **Sir Isaac Newton's thirst for knowledge was applied to all aspects of science.**

What does the phrase "thirst for knowledge" refer to?

- Ⓐ The intelligence to understand difficult subjects
- Ⓑ A commitment to helping others learn
- Ⓒ The ability to absorb and remember information
- Ⓓ A desire to know everything

14 According to the passage, in which area did Sir Isaac Newton carry out his most important work?

- Ⓐ Mathematics
- Ⓑ Physics
- Ⓒ Theology
- Ⓓ Astronomy

15 How would this passage be different if it were an autobiography?

- Ⓐ It would be a more factual summary of Newton's theories.
- Ⓑ It would include references to prove the statements made.
- Ⓒ It would include quotes from other sources.
- Ⓓ It would be written by Isaac Newton himself.

16 Which paragraph has the main purpose of describing Sir Isaac Newton's contributions to physics? Circle the paragraph you have selected.

Paragraph 1   Paragraph 2   Paragraph 3

Paragraph 4   Paragraph 5   Paragraph 6

17 What is the main purpose of the information in the table? In your answer, explain how the information in the table relates to the rest of the passage.

_____

_____

_____

_____

_____

18 Give **two** details the author includes to support the idea that Sir Isaac Newton had a strong influence on science.

Supporting Detail 1:

_____

_____

Supporting Detail 2:

_____

_____

19 Complete the table below by listing **two** other fields of study and summarizing Newton's major achievements in the field.

Field of Study	Major Achievements
Physics	He developed the three laws of motions and was the first person to understand gravity.

Alexander Graham Bell

Alexander Graham Bell is a famous inventor. He was born in Scotland in 1847. Bell was always curious about how things worked and his first invention came at the age of just 12. After learning from a neighbor about the difficult process of dehusking wheat, Bell began working on a solution. He built a machine that would dehusk wheat much more easily. His neighbor thanked him by allowing him to use one of his workshops to invent in.

While Bell invented many things, he is best known for inventing the telephone. His interest in sound also began when he was young. His mother suffered from hearing loss and gradually became deaf. This prompted Bell to become interested in speech, sounds, and hearing. Bell continued experimenting with sound, which eventually led to experiments involving sending sounds over wires. On March 7, 1876, Bell was awarded the patent for his method and apparatus of sending sounds telegraphically. It wasn't until a few days after the patent was awarded that he actually got it to work. On March 10, 1876, Bell successfully transmitted clear speech in both directions. The telephone was born.

By 1886, over 150,000 homes in America had telephones. The following years saw his creation become used worldwide. Telephones quickly became a normal part of life and something that most people viewed as necessary.

Bell disliked the attention that his invention brought to him. Even though he invented it, he disliked telephones. He preferred to be left alone and not bothered. He did not even have a telephone in his place of work. He died in August, 1922.

Poor Elisha Gray

At the same time that Bell was developing his telephone, an inventor named Elisha Gray was developing his. Gray applied for a patent on his invention on the same day as Bell. However, Gray applied several hours after Bell. Alexander Graham Bell was awarded the patent for the first telephone. If Elisha Gray had been just a few hours quicker, he would be much more well known today.

20 Which detail about Alexander Graham Bell would be least important to include in a summary of his life?

　Ⓐ　He was born in Scotland in 1847.

　Ⓑ　He is best known for inventing the telephone.

　Ⓒ　He was awarded a patent for the telephone in 1876.

　Ⓓ　He did not have a telephone in his place of work.

21 The anecdote about Bell creating the dehusking machine mainly shows —

　Ⓐ　that Bell was a hard worker

　Ⓑ　that Bell was a good problem solver

　Ⓒ　that Bell could be lazy at times

　Ⓓ　that Bell cared for other people

22 How is the information in the passage mainly organized?

　Ⓐ　A problem is described and then a solution is given.

　Ⓑ　Events are described in the order they occurred.

　Ⓒ　An argument is made and then facts are given.

　Ⓓ　The first telephone is compared to telephones today.

23 Elisha Gray is probably referred to as "Poor Elisha Gray" to show he —

　Ⓐ　had no money

　Ⓑ　was unlucky

　Ⓒ　did not work hard enough

　Ⓓ　created a bad design

24 How do you think Elisha Gray would have felt when Alexander Graham Bell was awarded the patent for the first telephone?

_____

_____

_____

_____

_____

25 List **two** details the author includes to show the success of the telephone.

1: _____

_____

2: _____

_____

26 The passages all describe a person who made major achievements in their fields by developing new ideas or inventing something new. Write an essay in which you describe the personal qualities that it takes to invent or develop something new.

- In your essay, describe one or two personal qualities that you think people need to invent or develop something new.
- Describe how Mark Zuckerberg, Isaac Newton, and Alexander Graham Bell have the qualities you have identified.

END OF SET 2

IAR Practice

Set 3

Literary Text with Narrative Writing Task

Instructions

This set has one passage for you to read. The passage is followed by questions.

Read each question carefully. For each multiple-choice question, fill in the circle for the correct answer. For other types of questions, follow the instructions given. Some of the questions require a written answer. Write your answer on the lines provided.

The last question requires you to write a story. Write your answer on the lines provided.

Spinning the Spider's Web

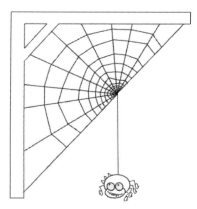
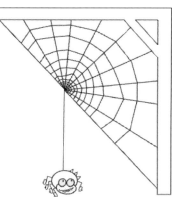

The spider spins his silken web,
In the corner of my home,
He weaves it for his family,
One teeny space their own.

I watch him as he toils,
Through the hours of the day,
Spinning as the summer burns,
Forever building come what may.

And when his web is broken,
He never sheds a tear,
He simply spins and starts again,
And keeps his loved ones near.

This small kingdom is his castle,
And a tiny place to rest,
Although some may beg to differ,
He builds his home to be the best.

He goes about his business,
And does not seek to pry or scare,
He means no harm to those around him,
To cross your path, he wouldn't dare.

The spider just keeps on spinning,
His winding, silken web,
Building homes amongst the darkness,
Keeping family in good stead.

So next time you see the spider,
Spinning webs inside your home,
Think how hard he has to toil,
Without a single word or moan.

1. Read this line from the poem.

   I watch him as he toils,

   What does the word <u>toils</u> mean?
   - Ⓐ Works
   - Ⓑ Spins
   - Ⓒ Struggles
   - Ⓓ Plays

2. Read this line from the poem.

   One teeny space their own.

   Complete the chart by dividing the words listed below into synonyms of <u>teeny</u> and antonyms of <u>teeny</u>.

   tiny   giant   small   massive

   little   huge   great   minute

Synonyms	Antonyms

3 What does the poet seem to find most impressive about spiders?

Ⓐ That they can live anywhere

Ⓑ That they never stop working

Ⓒ That they are not afraid of anything

Ⓓ That they leave people alone

4 Think about your answer to Question 3. Write **two** lines below that support your answer to Question 3. Explain what each line shows about the poet's opinion of spiders.

Line 1: _____

_____

_____

Line 2: _____

_____

_____

5 Which stanza of the poem has a message about facing disappointments?

Ⓐ Stanza 1

Ⓑ Stanza 2

Ⓒ Stanza 3

Ⓓ Stanza 4

6 Based on your answer to Question 5, explain how the poet communicates the message about overcoming disappointments.

_____

_____

_____

_____

_____

7 Which literary technique does the poet use in the first line of the poem?

Ⓐ   Alliteration

Ⓑ   Simile

Ⓒ   Metaphor

Ⓓ   Flashback

8 What is the rhyme pattern of each stanza of the poem?

Ⓐ   All the lines rhyme with each other.

Ⓑ   There are two pairs of rhyming lines.

Ⓒ   The second and fourth lines rhyme.

Ⓓ   None of the lines rhyme.

9 Which statement would the poet most likely agree with?

- Ⓐ People should make their own homes like spiders do.
- Ⓑ People should keep their homes free from spider webs.
- Ⓒ People should be aware of the dangers of spiders.
- Ⓓ People should leave spiders alone.

10 The poet states that "to cross your path, he wouldn't dare." What does the phrase "cross your path" refer to?

- Ⓐ Scaring someone
- Ⓑ Running into someone
- Ⓒ Stealing from someone
- Ⓓ Arguing with someone

11 Describe what people can learn from the spider about hard work and determination.

_____

_____

_____

_____

_____

12 Select the line from the poem that contains a metaphor.

☐ *I watch him as he toils,*

☐ *Through the hours of the day,*

☐ *He simply spins and starts again,*

☐ *This small kingdom is his castle,*

☐ *He builds his home to be the best.*

☐ *His winding, silken web,*

☐ *So next time you see the spider,*

☐ *Think how hard he has to toil,*

13 Describe the meaning of the metaphor identified in Question 12. In your answer, explain what the metaphor shows about the spider's home.

_____

_____

_____

_____

_____

_____

14 Imagine what it is like to be the spider. Write a story from the point of view of the spider describing **one** of the events below in the spider's life.

- when the web breaks and he has to start again
- when he finally finishes spinning the web
- when he sees a person worrying about him and his web

In your story, tell what the spider does and how the spider feels.

_____

_____

_____

_____

_____

_____

_____

_____

_____

_____

_____

END OF SET 3

IAR Practice

Set 4

Short Informational Text

Instructions

This set has one passage for you to read. The passage is followed by questions.

Read each question carefully. For each multiple-choice question, fill in the circle for the correct answer. For other types of questions, follow the instructions given. Some of the questions require a written answer. Write your answer on the lines provided.

To My Teacher

June 15, 2018

Dear Miss Hooper,

I am writing to thank you for the help you have given me this year. We have covered many subjects in class and you have helped me with every single one. You explain things so clearly, and are also amazingly patient. I really believe you have a great skill for teaching others. Without your assistance, I would of struggled to do as well as I have. You should be very proud of the way that you help children to learn. It is because of you that I am thinking about becoming a teacher when I am older.

There were so many highlights this year. Whatever the subject, you made it fun and interesting to everyone. All of your students found learning new things so easy because of you. You never once made me feel silly for asking a question. You were always willing to explain something again and again until I understood.

I have mixed feelings about school next year. Firstly, I guess I am sad that you will no longer be my teacher. However, I am pleased that other children will get to share your knowledge. It would be selfish for me to keep you to myself all through school! I hope that they thank you for the good work that you do. You deserve it and it is the least we can do.

I did not enjoy school much before this year. I was new to the school this year. At my old school, I found learning difficult and quite a challenge. It made me so nervous about starting a new school, but the change turned out to be a huge blessing. The last nine months have changed everything. I am now very confident and looking forward to the next school year.

Thank you once again. You have truly been a great teacher and helped me greatly. I hope that we may even share the same classroom again one day.

Yours sincerely,

Jacob Maclean

1   Read this sentence from the letter.

   There were so many highlights this year.

   What does the word <u>highlights</u> refer to?
   - Ⓐ   The best parts
   - Ⓑ   Challenges
   - Ⓒ   Breakthroughs
   - Ⓓ   Main ideas

2   Circle the **two** words from the passage that have about the same meaning.

   help   pleased   interesting   selfish

   fun   difficult   assistance   proud

3   Which sentence from the passage is a fact?
   - Ⓐ   *Whatever the subject, you made it fun and interesting to everyone.*
   - Ⓑ   *I really believe you have a great skill for teaching others.*
   - Ⓒ   *You should be very proud of the way that you help children to learn.*
   - Ⓓ   *I was new to the school this year.*

4 What is the main reason Jacob wrote the letter?

   Ⓐ   To tell how he wants to become a teacher

   Ⓑ   To explain that he is leaving the teacher's class

   Ⓒ   To express his thanks to his teacher

   Ⓓ   To encourage his teacher to keep working hard

5 Which sentence best summarizes the main idea of the letter?

   Ⓐ   *It is because of you that I am thinking about becoming a teacher when I am older.*

   Ⓑ   *I have mixed feelings about school next year.*

   Ⓒ   *I did not enjoy school much before this year.*

   Ⓓ   *You have truly been a great teacher and helped me greatly.*

6 Jacob describes Miss Hooper as "amazingly patient." Describe **two** details given in the passage that show her patience.

   1: _____

      _____

   2: _____

      _____

7 How does Jacob feel about not having Miss Hooper as his teacher next year?

    Ⓐ   Upset and angry

    Ⓑ   Pleased and excited

    Ⓒ   Sad, but understanding

    Ⓓ   Confused, but unconcerned

8 Based on your answer to Question 7, explain how you can tell that Jacob feels this way.

_____

_____

_____

_____

_____

9 Which detail best explains why Jacob appreciates Miss Hooper so much?

    Ⓐ   After this year, Jacob will not be taught by Miss Hooper.

    Ⓑ   Before Miss Hooper, Jacob always found learning difficult.

    Ⓒ   During the year, Jacob struggled more than all the other students.

    Ⓓ   At his last school, Jacob was bored and made little effort.

10   Select **all** the statements that are effects Miss Hooper had on Jacob.

☐   Making him look forward to school next year

☐   Making him want to become a teacher

☐   Making him want to join more school clubs

☐   Helping him learn more

☐   Helping him make new friends

☐   Helping him become more confident

11   Jacob states that starting a new school "turned out to be a huge blessing." Explain why Jacob feels this way.

_____

_____

_____

_____

_____

12 Look at the chart below.

Why Jacob Thinks Miss Hooper is a Good Teacher

1) She is patient.
2)
3)

Complete the chart by writing **two** of the sentences below in the empty spaces.

She is funny.   She is well-trained.   She explains things clearly.
She is proud.   She makes class fun.   She gives challenging work.

13 Read this paragraph from the passage.

> **Thank you once again. You have truly been a great teacher and helped me greatly. I hope that we may even share the same classroom again one day.**

How does this paragraph relate to the ideas of the rest of the passage?

Ⓐ   It introduces new ideas.

Ⓑ   It presents evidence against the main ideas.

Ⓒ   It restates the main ideas.

Ⓓ   It gives details to support the main ideas.

14 Think about how Jacob describes Miss Hooper. Choose the **one** quality Miss Hooper has that you think is most important for a good teacher. Explain why you chose that quality and why it is most important.

END OF SET 4

IAR Practice

Set 5

Short Literary Text

> **Instructions**
>
> This set has one passage for you to read. The passage is followed by questions.
>
> Read each question carefully. For each multiple-choice question, fill in the circle for the correct answer. For other types of questions, follow the instructions given. Some of the questions require a written answer. Write your answer on the lines provided.

Little White Lily
By George Macdonald

1. Little White Lily
Sat by a stone,
Drooping and waiting
Till the sun shone.

2. Little White Lily
Sunshine has fed;
Little White Lily
Is lifting her head.

3. Little White Lily
Said: "It is good
Little White Lily's
Clothing and food."

4. Little White Lily
Dressed like a bride!
Shining with whiteness,
And crowned beside!

5. Little White Lily
Drooping with pain,
Waiting and waiting
For the wet rain.

6. Little White Lily
Holdeth her cup;
Rain is fast falling
And filling it up.

7. Little White Lily
Said: "Good again,
When I am thirsty
To have the nice rain.

8. Now I am stronger,
Now I am cool;
Heat cannot burn me,
My veins are so full."

9. Little White Lily
Smells very sweet;
On her head sunshine,
Rain at her feet.

10. Thanks to the sunshine,
Thanks to the rain,
Little White Lily
Is happy again.

1   Read these lines from the poem.

> **Little White Lily**
> **Is happy again.**

Which literary device does the poet use in these lines?

Ⓐ   Simile

Ⓑ   Metaphor

Ⓒ   Personification

Ⓓ   Hyperbole

2   Based on your answer to Question 1, explain how the literary device helps readers connect with the poem.

_____

_____

_____

_____

_____

3 Based on the poem, what is most important to the lily?

- Ⓐ Having water
- Ⓑ Smelling nice
- Ⓒ Being appreciated
- Ⓓ Getting shelter

4 What is the rhyme pattern of each stanza of the poem?

- Ⓐ The second and fourth lines rhyme.
- Ⓑ There are two pairs of rhyming lines.
- Ⓒ The first and last lines rhyme.
- Ⓓ None of the lines rhyme.

5 Select **all** the lines below that contain alliteration.

- ☐ *Sat by a stone,*
- ☐ *Drooping and waiting*
- ☐ *Sunshine has fed;*
- ☐ *Shining with whiteness,*
- ☐ *Rain is fast falling*
- ☐ *Heat cannot burn me,*
- ☐ *Thanks to the rain,*

6 Which of the following is used throughout the poem?

   Ⓐ   Symbolism, using an object to stand for something else

   Ⓑ   Hyperbole, using exaggeration to make a point

   Ⓒ   Repetition, repeating words, phrases, or lines

   Ⓓ   Flashback, referring back to an event in the past

7 Why does the poet compare the lily to a bride?

   Ⓐ   To show how special the lily feels

   Ⓑ   To emphasize how white the lily is

   Ⓒ   To explain that the lily is being used in a wedding

   Ⓓ   To suggest that the lily moves slowly

8 Read these lines from the poem.

   Little White Lily
   Drooping with pain,
   Waiting and waiting
   For the wet rain.

   These lines suggest that the lily feels —

   Ⓐ   confident

   Ⓑ   desperate

   Ⓒ   calm

   Ⓓ   angry

9   In which stanza does the lily feel about the same as in the first stanza? Circle the stanza you have chosen.

   Stanza 2   Stanza 3   Stanza 4   Stanza 5   Stanza 6

   Stanza 7   Stanza 8   Stanza 9   Stanza 10

10 Think about how the lily feels in the first stanza and the stanza you identified in Question 9. Compare and contrast why the lily feels that way in each stanza.

   _____

   _____

   _____

   _____

   _____

11 The poet probably uses the word <u>drooping</u> in the first paragraph to create a sense of –

   Ⓐ   determination

   Ⓑ   sadness

   Ⓒ   loneliness

   Ⓓ   relaxation

12 Read these lines from the poem.

> **Little White Lily**
> **Holdeth her cup;**
> **Rain is fast falling**
> **And filling it up.**

Explain what these lines are describing. Why can what is described not happen until the sun is shining?

_____

_____

_____

_____

_____

13 Complete the table below by listing **two** stanzas that include dialogue. For each stanza, describe what the dialogue tells the reader.

Stanza	What the Dialogue Tells the Reader

14 Explain how the weather affects the lily. Use details from the poem in your answer.

END OF SET 5

IAR Practice

Set 6

Long Informational Text

Instructions

This set has one passage for you to read. The passage is followed by questions.

Read each question carefully. For each multiple-choice question, fill in the circle for the correct answer. For other types of questions, follow the instructions given. Some of the questions require a written answer. Write your answer on the lines provided.

Manchester United Soccer Club

About Soccer

1. Soccer is a ball sport that was invented in England in the 1800s. It is an outdoor sport. An individual match sees two teams of 11 players compete against each other. The object of the game is to work the ball into one of the two goals positioned at each end of the field.

2. It is a sport that is played all over the world. It is most popular in South America and Europe. The most successful international team is Brazil. They have won five World Cups since 1930, which is a competition that is held every 4 years. Italy has won four World Cups. Germany is not far behind, with three wins.

3. Soccer is not as popular as sports like baseball and football in the United States. The 2013 championship match of Major League Soccer in America had a crowd of 21,650. This is much less than for the Super Bowl, which had 71,000 people. However, soccer is a very entertaining sport to watch. Soccer may become a favorite sport in the United States one day.

4. As with popular American sports, major teams enjoy the massive support of their fans. Manchester United Soccer Club is based in the United Kingdom and is one of the most-loved teams. The love that fans have of the team is based on their long history, their success, and the talented and popular players that have been part of the team.

A Famous Soccer Club

5. Manchester United is a famous soccer team. They are based in the United Kingdom. They play in the English Premier League and the European Champions League. They are known as one of the most successful soccer clubs in the world.

6. They were first formed in 1888. At this time, they were named the Newton Heath Football Club. In 1901, they were sold and were given the new name of Manchester United.

7. They are the most successful club in the English League. They have won the English Premier League nineteen times. This is one more than their nearest rivals, Liverpool.

8. Since 1958, Manchester United have also won the European Champions League three times. This competition features teams from across Europe. It is this success that has helped them become such a well-known team.

9. David Beckham is one of the club's most famous players. He played for Manchester United from 1993 until 2003. In this time, he scored 62 goals for the club and helped his team win eight championships. He scored some amazing goals, including one from the halfway line that floated above the goalkeeper's head and curved into the net. The goal became so famous that it was voted by the British public as number 18 on a list of 100 greatest sporting moments. Beckham was known for being able to curve or bend the ball. It allowed him to score some amazing goals. These thrilled fans and helped draw huge crowds to games.

©Wikimedia Commons

10. In 2007, Beckham made an unexpected move. He joined America's Major League Soccer, and began playing for Los Angeles Galaxy. He was paid around $6.5 million per year. One of the most interesting things about the deal was that Beckham was not just paid by the Los Angeles Galaxy team. He was also paid by all the teams in America's Major League Soccer. The teams agreed to this because they hoped that having such a major star in their league would attract more people to the sport.

Manchester United's English Premier League Grand Final Wins

Year	Team Defeated
1908	Aston Villa
1911	Aston Villa
1952	Tottenham
1956	Blackpool
1957	Tottenham
1965	Leeds United
1967	Nottingham Forest
1993	Aston Villa
1994	Blackburn Rovers
1996	Newcastle United
1997	Newcastle United
1999	Arsenal
2000	Arsenal
2001	Arsenal
2003	Arsenal
2007	Chelsea
2008	Chelsea
2009	Chelsea
2011	Chelsea

1 Which meaning of the word <u>object</u> is used in the sentence below?

> **The object of the game is to work the ball into one of the two goals positioned at each end of the field.**

- Ⓐ A goal or aim
- Ⓑ A type of item
- Ⓒ To argue against
- Ⓓ To refuse to do something

2 Which detail from the passage is an opinion?

- Ⓐ Soccer was invented in the 1800s.
- Ⓑ Soccer is an outdoor sport.
- Ⓒ Soccer teams have 11 players each.
- Ⓓ Soccer is entertaining to watch.

3 Complete the table by adding information about the **three** most successful international teams. Order the teams from most to least successful.

Most Successful International Teams	Number of World Cup Wins Since 1930
1.	
2.	
3.	

4 Where was the game of soccer invented?

  Ⓐ England

  Ⓑ Brazil

  Ⓒ Italy

  Ⓓ Germany

5 Draw lines to match each sentence in paragraph 3 with the best description of the sentence. The first sentence has been matched for you.

Sentence	Description
Soccer is not as popular as sports like baseball and football in the United States.	a prediction
The 2013 championship match of Major League Soccer in America had a crowd of 21,650.	the main claim
This is much less than for the Super Bowl, which had 71,000 people.	an opinion
However, soccer is a very entertaining sport to watch.	a comparison
Soccer may become a favorite sport in the United States one day.	a fact given to support a claim

(The first sentence is matched to "the main claim.")

6 Circle the **two** words from the passage that have about the same meaning.

    formed   rivals   success   competition

    famous   teams   named   well-known

7 Which sentence is best supported by the information in the table at the end of the passage?

  Ⓐ *They have won the English Premier League nineteen times.*

  Ⓑ *This is one more than their nearest rivals, Liverpool.*

  Ⓒ *Since 1958, Manchester United have also won the European Champions League three times.*

  Ⓓ *This competition features teams from across Europe.*

8 Write F next to the sentences that are facts. Write O next to the sentences that are opinions.

    ___ They are based in the United Kingdom.

    ___ In 1901, they were sold and were given the new name of Manchester United.

    ___ Since 1958, Manchester United have also won the European Champions League three times.

    ___ It is this success that has helped them become such a well-known team.

9   List **two** facts the author includes to show that Manchester United have been a successful team.

1: _____

_____

2: _____

_____

10   Paragraph 10 describes how David Beckham was paid by all the teams in America's Major League Soccer. Which idea from "About Soccer" does this detail best support?

- Ⓐ   Soccer is played all over the world.
- Ⓑ   Soccer is not as popular in America as other sports.
- Ⓒ   Soccer teams in Europe enjoy massive support from their fans.
- Ⓓ   Soccer is played by teams of 11 players.

11   What is the main purpose of the seventh and eighth paragraphs?

- Ⓐ   To describe how the team formed
- Ⓑ   To describe the team's achievements
- Ⓒ   To explain why the team is successful
- Ⓓ   To show that the team has improved over time

12 Complete the chart below by writing the correct number in each empty box.

Team	Number of Times Defeated by Manchester United in the English Premier League Final
Aston Villa	
Arsenal	
Tottenham	

13 Read this dictionary entry for the word deal.

> **deal** *noun*
> 1. a business agreement 2. a bargain 3. the treatment given to somebody 4. the distribution of cards

Now read this sentence from the passage.

> **One of the most interesting things about the deal was that Beckham was not just paid by the Los Angeles Galaxy team.**

Which definition of the word deal is used in the sentence above?

Ⓐ Definition 1

Ⓑ Definition 2

Ⓒ Definition 3

Ⓓ Definition 4

14 The author states that the popularity of Manchester United is partly based on "the talented players that have been part of the team." How does the information given about David Beckham support this statement? Use information from the passage to support your answer.

END OF SET 6

IAR Practice

Set 7

Paired Literary Passages

Instructions

This set has two short passages for you to read. Read each passage and answer the questions that follow it.

For each multiple-choice question, fill in the circle for the correct answer. For other types of questions, follow the instructions given. Some of the questions require a written answer. Write your answer on the lines provided.

After reading both passages, you will use information from both passages to answer a question. Write your answer on the lines provided.

A New Start

August 2, 2018

Dear Aunt Jamie,

What a day! I started at my new school this morning and had the best time. I made lots of new friends and really liked my teachers. I was so nervous the night before, but I had no reason to be. Everyone was so friendly and polite. They made me feel at ease. It was like I'd been at the school for a hundred years!

The day started very early at exactly 7 o'clock. I didn't want to feel rushed, so I made sure to get up early. I had my breakfast downstairs with my mom. She could tell that I was very anxious. Mom kept asking me what was wrong. I admitted that I was scared that people wouldn't like me or that everyone would just ignore me. She told me I had nothing to worry about and that everyone was going to love me. If they didn't love me, Mom said to send them her way for a good talking to. I couldn't stop laughing.

My mom dropped me off at the school gates about ten minutes before the bell. A little blond girl got dropped off at the same time and started waving at me. She ran over and told me her name was Abigail. She was very nice and we became close straight away. We spent all morning together and began to chat to another girl called Stacey. The three of us sat together in class all day and we even made our way home together! It went so quickly. Our teacher told us that tomorrow we would really start learning and developing new skills.

It is late now so I am going to sleep, but I cannot wait until tomorrow! I feel as though I am really going to enjoy my time at my new school. I only hope that my new friends feel the same way too.

Lots of love,

Casey

1   Which of these is the opening of the letter?

    Ⓐ   *A New Start*

    Ⓑ   *August 2, 2018*

    Ⓒ   *Dear Aunt Jamie,*

    Ⓓ   *Lots of love,*

2   Read this statement from the first paragraph of the letter.

    What a day!

    Circle the emotion that best describes what Casey uses this statement to show. Then explain how the details in the first paragraph helped you choose your answer.

    nervousness   excitement   surprise   relief

    _____
    _____
    _____
    _____
    _____

3 Read this sentence from the letter.

She was very nice and we became close straight away.

What does Casey mean when she says that they "became close"?

Ⓐ They began to be friends.

Ⓑ They walked near each other.

Ⓒ They stayed on their own.

Ⓓ They were in the same class.

4 What will Casey most likely do when she arrives at school the next day?

Ⓐ Sit by herself in the playground

Ⓑ See if there are any other new people

Ⓒ Look for Abigail and Stacey

Ⓓ Go to class early to see her teacher

5 Which word means the opposite of <u>polite</u>?

Ⓐ Rude

Ⓑ Nice

Ⓒ Easygoing

Ⓓ Calm

6 The reader can tell that Casey's mother –

    Ⓐ   is used to meeting new people

    Ⓑ   is very worried about her daughter

    Ⓒ   cares about Casey's feelings

    Ⓓ   wishes Casey did not have to start a new school

7 Based on your answer to Question 6, describe how Casey's mother's actions show what she is like.

_____

_____

_____

_____

_____

8 Which word would Casey most likely use to describe Abigail?

    Ⓐ   Funny

    Ⓑ   Friendly

    Ⓒ   Bossy

    Ⓓ   Shy

9 Casey writes that "It was like I'd been at the school for a hundred years!" What is this an example of?

- Ⓐ Imagery, using details to create an image or picture
- Ⓑ Hyperbole, using exaggeration to make a point
- Ⓒ Flashback, describing events that occurred far in the past
- Ⓓ Symbolism, using an object to stand for something else

10 Think about your answer to Question 9. What is the statement Casey makes used to show?

- Ⓐ How bored Casey is
- Ⓑ How comfortable Casey feels
- Ⓒ How there is too much new information to take in
- Ⓓ How the school has a long history

11 How is Casey's day different from what she expected? Use details from the passage to support your answer.

_____

_____

_____

_____

_____

A New Arrival

Today was a very exciting day for me and my family. It was the day that my new baby brother came home from the hospital.

I remember when I first learned that I was going to have a new baby brother. "I have great news Emma," my mother said. "You are going to be a big sister." I just stared at my mother and I didn't even smile. I really wasn't sure what to think, but I had all these thoughts running through my head. I worried that he would drive me crazy by crying all the time. I worried that my parents might want him to have my room. I even worried that Mom would be too busy to come and watch me at my dance competitions.

All those things I worried about seem ridiculous now. I soon forgot about most of them anyway. By the time he was ready to arrive, I didn't have a single worry. I was far too excited about getting to meet him. I was looking forward to being his big sister and helping to look after him.

My baby brother was born yesterday morning at 9:51. My father came home in the afternoon and was overjoyed. He weighed 8 pounds and 1 ounce and my parents named him Bradley. My dad says that he is the most beautiful baby. I could barely sleep the night before. I was so excited about Bradley coming home. Eventually, I drifted off to sleep just as the morning sun began to rise.

I woke up as usual today at 9 o'clock. I went downstairs and enjoyed some toast for breakfast. I knew that my father was collecting my mother and Bradley at 11:30. I watched TV for a while before trying to read one of my favorite books. Whatever I tried to do, I just could not take my mind off my newborn brother. I couldn't help but try to imagine what he must look like. In my mind, he had bright blond hair and sparkling blue eyes. I wondered whether he would understand who I was when he first saw me. My daydreaming was interrupted by my dad's voice. "Let's go Emma," he called. It was finally time to leave.

I headed out to the car and we drove toward the hospital. I couldn't stop talking as we made our way through the winding roads. The short trip to the hospital seemed to take forever. We finally arrived at the hospital. We made our way through the reception and headed to the maternity ward. As we arrived at the doors, I could see my mother at the far end. She held a small bundle wrapped in a blue blanket in her arms.

Mom just smiled as I reached the end of her bed. She looked tired but extremely happy. I just stared for a few moments before Mom asked me if I wanted to meet my brother! I couldn't stop smiling and reached out in an instant. Mom held out her arms and passed Bradley to me.

I took him in my arms and cradled his tiny little baby body. As I looked down, he slowly opened his eyes and gazed up at me. They were the deepest blue that anyone could ever imagine. As I stroked his face he began to smile softly. Dad told me that he looks just like me when I was born. The thought that I was ever that beautiful made me smile. Then Bradley slowly closed his eyes and drifted off to sleep.

12 Which word best describes the tone of the sentence below?

I took him in my arms and cradled his tiny little baby body.

- Ⓐ Loving
- Ⓑ Casual
- Ⓒ Lively
- Ⓓ Serious

13 Which word means about the same as <u>overjoyed</u>?

My father came home in the afternoon and was overjoyed.

- Ⓐ Tired
- Ⓑ Delighted
- Ⓒ Relaxed
- Ⓓ Gloomy

14 Why does Emma most likely say that the trip to the hospital "seemed to take forever"?

- Ⓐ Her father got lost on the way.
- Ⓑ She was nervous about seeing her brother.
- Ⓒ She was excited and impatient.
- Ⓓ She lived far from the hospital.

15 Read this sentence from the passage.

> **They were the deepest blue that anyone could ever imagine.**

Which literary device is used in the sentence?

- Ⓐ Alliteration, using words with the same consonant sounds
- Ⓑ Hyperbole, using exaggeration to make a point
- Ⓒ Simile, comparing two items using the words "like" or "as"
- Ⓓ Symbolism, using an object to stand for something else

16 Which of these would Emma probably most look forward to doing the next day?

- Ⓐ Reading her favorite book
- Ⓑ Chatting with her father
- Ⓒ Watching television
- Ⓓ Rocking her brother to sleep

17 Which **two** words would Emma most likely use to describe her day? Tick the boxes of the words you have chosen.

- ☐ eerie
- ☐ surprising
- ☐ annoying
- ☐ disappointing
- ☐ special
- ☐ dull
- ☐ strange
- ☐ unforgettable

18 Which paragraph contains a flashback? Circle your choice. Then explain the purpose of the flashback.

| Paragraph 1 | Paragraph 2 | Paragraph 3 | Paragraph 4 |
| Paragraph 5 | Paragraph 6 | Paragraph 7 | Paragraph 8 |

_____

_____

_____

_____

_____

19 How can you tell that the author is excited about having a baby brother? Use at least **two** details from the passage in your answer.

_____

_____

_____

_____

_____

_____

20 Emma's first reaction to finding out she is going to have a brother can be described as selfish. List **two** details from the passage that show this.

1: _____

_____

2: _____

_____

21 Complete the web below by adding **three** more phrases from the paragraph below that create a sense of calm.

> I took him in my arms and cradled his tiny little baby body. As I looked down, he slowly opened his eyes and gazed up at me. They were the deepest blue that anyone could ever imagine. As I stroked his face he began to smile softly. Dad told me that he looks just like me when I was born. The thought that I was ever that beautiful made me smile. Then Bradley slowly closed his eyes and drifted off to sleep.

- stroked his face
- [ ]
- Phrases that Create a Sense of Calm
- [ ]
- [ ]

22 How do the experiences of Casey and Emma show that there is no need to be afraid of change? Use details from both passages in your answer.

END OF SET 7

IAR Practice

Set 8

Literary Texts with Writing Task

Instructions

This set has two passages for you to read. Read each passage and answer the questions that follow it.

For each multiple-choice question, fill in the circle for the correct answer. For other types of questions, follow the instructions given. Some of the questions require a written answer. Write your answer on the lines provided.

After reading both passages, you will answer an essay question. You will use information from both passages to answer this question. Write your answer on the lines provided.

The Inventor

1) Scott had always been creative. Ever since he had been a child, he had loved to experiment with new ideas. As Scott had grown, his passion had only grown stronger. After attending university, Scott decided that he wanted to become an inventor. He used his studies in engineering to design and produce many brand new things. His friends thought that he was misguided.

2) "You cannot spend your life as an inventor," said his best friend Luke. "You will never have a steady income."

3) Luke worked as a bank manager and worried for his friend's future.

4) "Why don't you reconsider and get a job in the city?" Luke often asked. "You can always invent on the weekends."

5) But Scott would not be distracted from his goals.

6) "This is my dream," he said to Luke. "I have wanted to be an inventor since I was a small child. I am not going to give up."

7) "But you might spend years trying and never make it," Luke said. "You don't want to look back and realize you wasted all your time and talent. You're a great engineer, so you know you could get a good job somewhere and do well for yourself."

8) Scott would explain that he didn't want to work making things that had already been invented. There was no challenge in that. He wanted to use his talents to create something new that would improve how things were done.

9) Luke would shrug and leave his friend to his many different projects. Over several years, Scott developed many ideas that failed to become a success. His first invention was a device that was designed to make a car use less fuel as it traveled. This had many flaws and Scott was unable to sell his invention.

10) His second idea was a special motorcycle helmet that provided better vision for riders. This invention received little support from people who worked in the industry. Scott's friend Luke continued to encourage him to find a different career.

11) "Scott, you have to think about your future. I am proud of you for trying so hard to follow your dreams. I think it is now time to try something else. If you don't, I worry about how things will turn out for you."

12) "Thank you Luke," Scott replied. "I appreciate it. But I cannot stop now. I am so close to coming up with something huge. If I left my designs now, all my life would have been wasted."

13) Luke nodded, "I understand my friend. Just know that I am here to support you."

14) Then one day it happened. Scott completed his design of a new wing for an airplane. It had taken six months. Scott's new invention would improve the efficiency of the plane. He presented it to several companies who all loved his idea. After some competition, a company offered to buy his idea and design plans. Scott accepted the offer.

15) "I knew that one day I would make it!" he said to Luke as they celebrated at his apartment.

16) Luke felt a little guilty for ever suggesting that Scott should give up.

17) "I don't know how you kept going all these years," Luke said. "You definitely deserve every bit of your success."

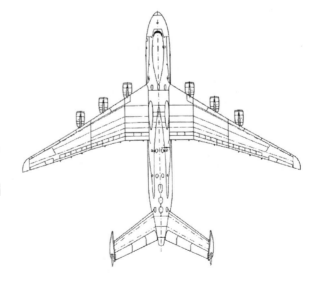

1 In the sentence below, which word could best be used in place of flaws?

This had many flaws and Scott was unable to sell his invention.

Ⓐ Costs

Ⓑ Faults

Ⓒ Benefits

Ⓓ Uses

2 Read this sentence from the passage.

As Scott had grown, his passion had only grown stronger.

The word passion shows that Scott is very –

Ⓐ enthusiastic

Ⓑ talented

Ⓒ impatient

Ⓓ knowledgeable

3 Which statement best describes how the photograph at the start of the passage relates to the information in the first paragraph?

Ⓐ It shows how Scott loved to experiment with new ideas.

Ⓑ It shows how Scott's passion increased as he got older.

Ⓒ It shows how Scott studied engineering at university.

Ⓓ It shows how Scott's goals were misguided.

4 According to the passage, what did Scott study at college?

- Ⓐ Science
- Ⓑ Mathematics
- Ⓒ Engineering
- Ⓓ Aviation

5 What type of passage is "The Inventor"?

- Ⓐ Realistic fiction
- Ⓑ Science fiction
- Ⓒ Biography
- Ⓓ Fable

6 Complete the table below by listing **two** reasons that Scott gives for continuing to chase his dream of being an inventor and **two** reasons that Luke gives for getting a regular job.

Scott's Reasons for Being an Inventor	Luke's Reasons for Getting a Regular Job

7 The main theme of the passage is about —

    Ⓐ   not giving up on your dreams

    Ⓑ   making the world a better place

    Ⓒ   improving on old ideas

    Ⓓ   making time for your friends

8 Based on your answer to Question 7, choose **two** paragraphs that support your answer. On the lines below, explain how each paragraph supports your answer.

Paragraph: _____

_____

_____

_____

_____

Paragraph: _____

_____

_____

_____

_____

9 Which word best describes Scott?

   Ⓐ   Foolish

   Ⓑ   Determined

   Ⓒ   Easygoing

   Ⓓ   Sensible

10 Based on your answer to Question 9, give **two** details from the passage that support your answer.

   1: _____

   _____

   2: _____

   _____

11 Circle **all** the words from the passage that contain prefixes.

creative	experiment	passion	stronger
university	misguided	reconsider	talent
projects	challenge	improve	different
unable	understand	competition	success

12 The table below describes Scott's inventions and their benefits. Complete the table using details from the passage.

Scott's Inventions

Invention	Benefit of the Invention
Device for a car	Reduced the amount of fuel used
Motorcycle helmet	
New airplane wing	

13 Do you think that Luke is a good friend to Scott? Explain why or why not.

_____

_____

_____

_____

_____

_____

The Aspiring Star

Troy longed to be a professional basketball player. He had loved the sport ever since he was a small child. He was also very skilled and fast on the basketball court. Despite this, he had one small problem. He was very short. His school coach had suggested that he would never make it in the professional leagues. Although he was devastated at first, he refused to give up on his dream.

Troy had several trials at professional clubs but failed to earn a contract. It was then that he attended the training ground of the Los Angeles Lakers. He asked the coach for a trial. As usual, he was refused. It wasn't in his nature just to walk away.

"But you haven't even given me a chance," said Troy.

"Why should I give you a shot?" asked the coach.

Troy paused before he answered.

"Because one day I am going to be the best player in the world and I will be able to help you out," he replied seriously.

The coach smiled at the confidence of the answer.

"Alright kid," he said. "I'll give you a chance to impress me."

Troy took part in a short practice match and was then allowed to showcase his individual skills. He knew he was being given a rare chance and he put everything he had into it. While the other players took a break for water, Troy stayed on the court and showed even more of his ball skills. He was one of the most skillful players on show and had the will to win to match. The coach was stunned.

"You certainly have a lot of talent for a little fellow," he said. "How would you like to sign on a youth contract?"

Troy agreed and was soon rising through the ranks. He was the shortest player by far, but he was also the hardest worker. He felt he had to work hard to overcome the natural height that he lacked. He practiced his ball skills far longer than everyone else. While he couldn't leap as high as everyone else, he was fast and could dribble the ball around everyone. It was rare to see Troy lose the ball or have it stolen from him. He often stole it from other players, and especially those who underestimated him.

Although some players continued to think he was too short to play, they soon changed their minds when they saw him in action. After two short years, he was a regular for the Lakers and had even won the award as the team's most valuable player. Even with Troy's help, the team was struggling. They were not winning many games and there were rumors that the coach was close to losing his job. It was before a game against the New York Jets that he called Troy into his office for a discussion.

"I have heard that if we lose tonight then I will be replaced as coach," he told Troy. "I need you to do more than play well tonight. I need you to carry the team and win the game. Do you remember your promise before I signed you?"

Troy nodded and smiled at his coach.

"You bet I do coach," he replied. "You bet I do."

Troy went on to play the game of his life that evening. The Lakers won the game and won every game that was left that season. The coach kept his job and led his team on to success.

14   Read this sentence from the passage.

> **Although he was devastated at first, he refused to give up on his dream.**

The word <u>devastated</u> means that Troy was –

- Ⓐ   understanding
- Ⓑ   very upset
- Ⓒ   not surprised
- Ⓓ   slightly amused

15   Read this sentence from the passage.

> **I need you to carry the team and win the game.**

What does the phrase "carry the team" refer to?

- Ⓐ   How Troy will have to cheer on his teammates
- Ⓑ   How Troy will have to do extra work
- Ⓒ   How Troy will have to motivate the team
- Ⓓ   How Troy will have to go against his team

16 What is the main hurdle that makes it difficult for Troy to play at a high level? How does Troy make up for it?

_____

_____

_____

_____

_____

17 Which statement best describes the theme of the passage?

Ⓐ It is important to keep your promises.

Ⓑ You can achieve your dreams if you work hard enough.

Ⓒ Confidence is the key to being great.

Ⓓ There is no time like the present.

18 In the third paragraph, Troy asks to be given a chance. How does this affect the rest of the events?

Ⓐ It proves to the coach that Troy is fearless enough to do well.

Ⓑ It helps Troy understand what it will take to achieve his goal.

Ⓒ It encourages the coach to be more open-minded about players.

Ⓓ It allows the coach to see how talented Troy is and get a contract.

19   Read this sentence from the end of the passage spoken by the coach.

Do you remember your promise before I signed you?

What promise is the coach referring to? Explain your answer.

_____

_____

_____

_____

_____

20   What is the point of view in the passage?

- Ⓐ   First person
- Ⓑ   Second person
- Ⓒ   Third person limited
- Ⓓ   Third person omniscient

21 How do you think the coach feels about his decision to give Troy a chance at the end of the passage? Use details from the passage to support your answer.

22 Troy's story can be described as inspiring. Explain why Troy's story is inspiring. Use details from the passage in your answer.

23 Complete the web below by listing **three** ways Troy's height actually helped him.

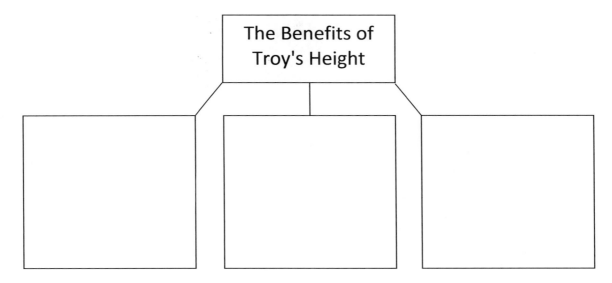

24 Describe **two** examples from the passage that show how Troy takes advantage of every chance he is given.

1: _____

_____

2: _____

_____

25 You have read two passages about people who did not give up on their goals. Write an essay that compares the characters Scott and Troy.

- In your answer, tell how Scott and Troy both do not give up on their goals.
- Describe the obstacles they each face.
- Explain how determination allows Scott and Troy to overcome the obstacles.
- Use details from both passages to support your answer.

_____

_____

_____

_____

_____

_____

_____

_____

_____

_____

_____

END OF SET 8

IAR Practice

Set 9

Informational Texts with Writing Task

Instructions

This set has three passages for you to read. Read each passage and answer the questions that follow it.

For each multiple-choice question, fill in the circle for the correct answer. For other types of questions, follow the instructions given. Some of the questions require a written answer. Write your answer on the lines provided.

After reading the three passages, you will answer an essay question. You will use information from all three passages to answer this question. Write your answer on the lines provided.

The Human Skeleton

Did you know that there are over 206 bones in the adult human skeleton? Newborn babies have over 270 bones. As a newborn baby grows, some of their bones are fused together.

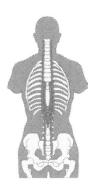

The skeleton performs several very important functions within our body. These include providing a support framework, protecting vital organs, and playing a crucial role in the generation of blood cells. Bones are also a storage site for many of the minerals our bodies need. It is important to keep your bones healthy so they can perform all these roles.

Osteoporosis is a medical condition that occurs when the bones become less dense. This makes them weak and brittle, and can lead to bones fracturing easily. When a bone is very brittle, something as simple as coughing can result in a fracture. Osteoporosis can affect anyone, but is most common in women. Luckily, preventing osteoporosis is quite simple. A diet high in calcium and sufficient exercise will usually prevent osteoporosis.

Three Simple Rules

1. Have a Diet High in Calcium
Your body needs calcium to keep your bones strong. Calcium is found in dairy products, leafy green vegetables, and soy products.

2. Get Enough Vitamin D
Your body uses sunlight to make vitamin D. As long as you spend a normal amount of time outdoors, your body should be getting enough vitamin D. Vitamin D is also found in salmon, tuna, and eggs.

3. Exercise
Regular exercise will keep your bones strong and healthy. Walking, running, jogging, or playing sports are all good for the health of your bones.

1. Choose **two** of the words below that are used in the passage. Explain how you can tell what each word chosen means by how it is used in the passage.

   fused   brittle   fracture   sufficient

   Word 1: _____

   _____

   _____

   _____

   Word 2: _____

   _____

   _____

   _____

2. Which two words from the passage have about the same meaning?
   - Ⓐ *storage, minerals*
   - Ⓑ *sunlight, outdoors*
   - Ⓒ *adult, newborn*
   - Ⓓ *vital, crucial*

3 Complete the web below using information from the passage.

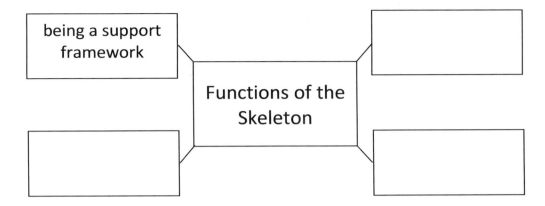

4 According to the passage, how are adults different from children?

Ⓐ They have more bones.

Ⓑ They have fewer bones.

Ⓒ Their bones have more purposes.

Ⓓ Their bones have fewer purposes.

5 What is the main reason the author begins the passage with a question?

Ⓐ To present a fact in a way that creates interest in the topic

Ⓑ To explain the main purpose of the article

Ⓒ To suggest that many people do not realize the importance of the skeleton

Ⓓ To encourage readers to research and find out more about the human skeleton

6 Which detail from the passage did you find most interesting or surprising? Explain why you found that detail interesting or surprising.

_____

_____

_____

_____

_____

7 What is the main purpose of the section titled "Three Simple Rules"? In your answer, explain how these rules relate to the rest of the passage.

_____

_____

_____

_____

_____

Food Poisoning

Bacteria grow quickly in the right conditions. When food isn't prepared, kept, or handled properly it has the potential to make you very ill. Food poisoning occurs when bacteria are introduced into food before it is eaten. Food poisoning can sometimes be as mild as having a stomachache, but it can also be much more serious. The Centers for Disease Control and Prevention (CDC) states that almost 50 million Americans get food poisoning every year. Of those, around 125,000 people are admitted to hospital and there are around 3,000 deaths. Luckily, food poisoning can be prevented. All you have to do is follow a few simple rules.

1: Wash your hands and the equipment you're going to use to prepare and serve the food.

2: Don't use the same chopping board for meat that you use to prepare fruit and vegetables. This is especially important if the fruit and vegetables are served raw.

3: Ensure your food is cooked thoroughly. The cooking process destroys most harmful bacteria, so this step can prevent food poisoning even when the raw food contains bacteria.

4: Properly store your food.

5: Make sure your refrigerator temperature is set low enough.

6: Follow the directions on packaging for how to store foods once they are open, and for how long to store food for.

7: Don't unfreeze and then refreeze food.

Top Tip

Many foods have to be used within a few days once they've been opened. It can be easy to forget when something was opened. Keep a marker near the fridge and write on the packaging what date the food was opened.

8 In rule 3, which word could best be used in place of <u>thoroughly</u>?

  Ⓐ Quickly

  Ⓑ Completely

  Ⓒ Cleanly

  Ⓓ Nicely

9 Which rule does the information in the box mainly relate to? Circle the answer you have chosen.

1   2   3   4   5   6   7

10 Based on your answer to Question 9, describe why you chose that rule. In your answer, explain how the rule and the information in the box relate to each other.

_____

_____

_____

_____

_____

11 What is the main purpose of the first paragraph?

    Ⓐ   To describe how to prevent food poisoning

    Ⓑ   To explain the importance of food safety

    Ⓒ   To encourage people to cook their own food

    Ⓓ   To show that bacteria can grow anywhere

12 Which of these rules from the passage best supports the conclusion that bacteria grow poorly in cold conditions?

    Ⓐ   *Don't use the same chopping board for chopping meat that you use to prepare fruit and vegetables.*

    Ⓑ   *Ensure your food is cooked thoroughly.*

    Ⓒ   *Make sure your refrigerator temperature is set low enough.*

    Ⓓ   *Don't unfreeze and then refreeze food.*

13 Describe **two** details the author includes to show the seriousness of food poisoning.

    1: _____

    _____

    2: _____

    _____

14 What is the cause of food poisoning? Use details from the passage to support your answer.

_____

_____

_____

_____

_____

15 Why do you think it is important not to use the same chopping board for meat that you use for fruit and vegetables? Explain your answer.

_____

_____

_____

_____

_____

Take a Deep Breath

The lung is an organ that is used to help many living things breathe. Humans have two lungs in their body. The lungs have several important purposes. The main purpose of the lungs is to take in oxygen from the air. Carbon dioxide leaves the body via the lungs. The lungs are also used to protect the heart from any sudden shocks to the chest. Another purpose of the lungs is to filter blood clots.

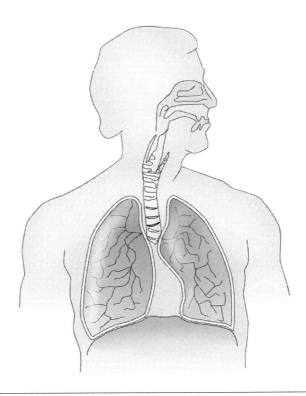

Looking After the Lungs

It is important to take good care of your lungs. One of the best ways to keep your lungs healthy is to exercise often. This gives your lungs a workout! The more you exercise, the stronger your lungs will become!

The lungs are so important that your body has built-in ways of protecting them. Have you ever breathed in dust? What happened? Have you heard of people who are affected by pollen in the air? If there is anything getting into the body from the air, your body has special ways of dealing with it. One way is to cough, which removes particles from the lungs and breathing passages. The other way is to sneeze, which removes particles from the nasal cavity and nose.

Sneezing is a bodily reflex similar to a cough. It serves the same purpose of a cough, which is to remove foreign bodies and irritants from the body. However, a sneeze is much more powerful than a cough. In fact, the air leaving the body from a sneeze can travel at speeds of up to 100 miles per hour!

A sneeze occurs when air is rapidly expelled, or removed from, the lungs. The scientific term for sneezing is sternutation. There are four main reasons that people sneeze.

- Irritation – people sneeze when something irritates the nose. This is the body's way of cleaning the nose and stopping irritants from getting into the lungs.
- Light – people can sneeze when they are suddenly exposed to bright light.
- Feeling full – some people have a very rare condition where they sneeze as a response to feeling very full after a meal.
- Infection – many infections by viruses, including the common cold, can cause people to sneeze. The purpose of the sneeze is to remove virus particles from the body.

The most common reason people sneeze is due to irritation. Many people sneeze when they breathe in dust, pollen, or other irritants. This condition is known as hay fever, and is most common in spring when there is a lot of pollen in the air.

For some people, spring flowers are a wonderful sign that the cold weather of winter and fall has passed. For others, flowers means the beginning of hay fever season.

16 Which sentence states the main idea of the first paragraph?

- Ⓐ *Humans have two lungs in their body.*
- Ⓑ *The lungs have several important purposes.*
- Ⓒ *Carbon dioxide leaves the body via the lungs.*
- Ⓓ *Another purpose of the lungs is to filter blood clots.*

17 What is the main purpose of the information in the box?

- Ⓐ To give advice on how to have healthy lungs
- Ⓑ To describe one of the purposes of the lungs
- Ⓒ To describe the two human lungs
- Ⓓ To show that lungs are important organs

18 Select **all** the statements below that are purposes of the lungs.

- ☐ Taking in oxygen
- ☐ Storing minerals
- ☐ Removing carbon dioxide
- ☐ Protecting the heart
- ☐ Filtering blood clots
- ☐ Making energy

19 How is the paragraph below mainly organized?

> **Sneezing is a bodily reflex similar to a cough. It serves the same purpose of a cough, which is to remove foreign bodies and irritants from the body. However, a sneeze is much more powerful than a cough. In fact, the air leaving the body from a sneeze can travel at speeds of up to 100 miles per hour!**

- Ⓐ A problem is described and then a solution is given.
- Ⓑ Events are described in the order they occur.
- Ⓒ Facts are given to support an argument.
- Ⓓ Two events are compared.

20 The photograph at the end of the passage mainly relates to which cause of sneezing?

- Ⓐ Irritation
- Ⓑ Light
- Ⓒ Feeling full
- Ⓓ Infection

21 How does the diagram help show how sneezing would clean the nose?

- Ⓐ It shows how the lungs can hold a lot of air.
- Ⓑ It shows how air only moves in one direction.
- Ⓒ It shows how quickly the air would be traveling.
- Ⓓ It shows how air from the lungs would travel through the nose.

22 Rank the following causes of sneezing from most common to least common. Write 1, 2, 3, and 4 on the lines to show your choices.

___ Irritation

___ Light

___ Feeling full

___ Infection

23 Which term best describes the sentence below?

The scientific term for sneezing is sternutation.

Ⓐ   Comparison

Ⓑ   Definition

Ⓒ   Exaggeration

Ⓓ   Assumption

24 Describe **two** ways that sneezing is different from coughing.

1: _____

_____

2: _____

_____

25 You have read three passages that relate to being healthy. The passages show how your body tries to keep you healthy and how you can keep healthy. Write an article for your school newspaper encouraging students to be healthy.

- In your article, describe how your body works to keep you healthy.
- Explain why it is important to help your body do its job.
- Describe what people can do to help stay healthy.

END OF SET 9

IAR Practice

Set 10

Literary Text with Narrative Writing Task

Instructions

This set has one passage for you to read. The passage is followed by questions.

Read each question carefully. For each multiple-choice question, fill in the circle for the correct answer. For other types of questions, follow the instructions given. Some of the questions require a written answer. Write your answer on the lines provided.

The last question requires you to write a story. Write your answer on the lines provided.

The Bees, the Wasps, and the Hornet

A store of honey had been found in a hollow tree. The wasps stated that it belonged to them. The bees were just as sure that the treasure was theirs. The argument grew very heated. It looked as if the affair could not be settled. But at last, with much good sense, they agreed to let a judge decide the matter. They brought the case before Judge Hornet.

When Judge Hornet called the case, witnesses stated that they had seen certain winged creatures in the neighborhood of the hollow tree. The creatures had hummed loudly, had striped bodies, and were yellow and black.

The wasps stated that this described them. The bees stated that this described them.

This did not help Judge Hornet make a decision. He said he wanted to take a few days to think about the case. When the case came up again, both sides had a large number of witnesses.

Judge Hornet sighed. He knew it was going to be a long day. Then the eldest bee asked if he could address the court.

"I'll allow it," Judge Hornet said.

"Your honor," the eldest bee said, "the case has now been going on for a week. If it is not decided soon, the honey will not be fit for anything. I move that the bees and the wasps be both instructed to make some honey. Then we shall soon see to whom the honey really belongs."

The wasps began to panic. They jumped up and down and complained loudly. Wise Judge Hornet quickly understood why they did so.

"It is clear," said Judge Hornet, "who made the honey and who could not have made it. The honey belongs to the bees."

1   Read this sentence from the passage.

   The argument grew very heated.

   The word <u>heated</u> suggests that the bees and wasps became —

   Ⓐ   confused

   Ⓑ   angry

   Ⓒ   warm

   Ⓓ   tired

2   In the sentence below, why does the author use the word <u>treasure</u>?

   The bees were just as sure that the treasure was theirs.

   Ⓐ   To suggest that the honey was gold

   Ⓑ   To show that the honey was hidden

   Ⓒ   To show that the honey had been there a long time

   Ⓓ   To suggest that the honey was precious

3   What is the main purpose of the first paragraph?

   Ⓐ   To describe the main problem

   Ⓑ   To compare the bees and the wasps

   Ⓒ   To introduce the setting

   Ⓓ   To describe how to solve an argument

4 The main lesson the wasps learn is about being —

    Ⓐ   hardworking

    Ⓑ   honest

    Ⓒ   prepared

    Ⓓ   skilled

5 Based on your answer to Question 4, explain how the outcome for the wasps shows the main lesson.

_____

_____

_____

_____

_____

6 How is the passage mainly organized?

    Ⓐ   Two events are compared and contrasted.

    Ⓑ   Events are described in the order they occur.

    Ⓒ   Facts are given to support an argument.

    Ⓓ   A question is asked and then answered.

7 Why do the wasps most likely panic when the elder bee suggests that the judge should instruct the bees and wasps to make honey?

- Ⓐ The wasps know they cannot make honey.
- Ⓑ The wasps are too tired to make honey.
- Ⓒ The wasps think the bees' honey will taste better.
- Ⓓ The wasps think it will take too long.

8 Explain what the judge decides when he sees the wasps panicking. Explain how the wasps' actions cause the judge to reach his decision.

_____

_____

_____

_____

_____

9 Based on his suggestion, the eldest bee is best described as —

- Ⓐ impatient
- Ⓑ polite
- Ⓒ wise
- Ⓓ cranky

10 The passage states that "when the case came up again, both sides had a large number of witnesses." How does this influence the events?

Ⓐ   It makes the wasps sorry for their actions because they realize how much the bees care about the honey.

Ⓑ   It makes the wasps upset and nervous because they fear being embarrassed in front of so many people.

Ⓒ   It makes the judge want to be sure to make the right decision because he knows how important it must be to both sides.

Ⓓ   It makes the judge open to listening to the ideas of the eldest bee because the judge wants to find a faster solution.

11 Complete the table below by describing **one** way the bees and the wasps are similar and **one** way the bees and the wasps are different. In the second column, describe how the similarity or difference affects the events of the passage.

Similarity	Effect on the Events
Difference	**Effect on the Events**

12 How can you tell that the events in the passage could not really happen? Use details from the passage in your answer.

_____

_____

_____

_____

_____

13 What is the main problem in the passage? How is the main problem solved? Use details from the passage to support your answer.

_____

_____

_____

_____

_____

14 In the passage, the wasps learn that it is does not pay to lie. Think about a time when you lied to get something you wanted. Write a story that tells about that time. In your story, describe why you lied and what happened after you lied.

END OF SET 10

IAR Practice

Set 11

Short Informational Text

Instructions

This set has one passage for you to read. The passage is followed by questions.

Read each question carefully. For each multiple-choice question, fill in the circle for the correct answer. For other types of questions, follow the instructions given. Some of the questions require a written answer. Write your answer on the lines provided.

Playing a Musical Instrument

Playing a musical instrument is a popular pastime for all age ranges. Young or old, it is lots of fun to play a musical instrument. There are many different types to choose from including guitar, flute, piano, trumpet, and saxophone.

Making a Choice

First, you need to choose a musical instrument that you would like to learn how to play. Here are some things you should think about:

- the cost of the instrument
- how easy or difficult the instrument is to learn
- whether there is a teacher available to help you learn it
- what opportunities there will be to play it

You might also think about the kind of music you'd like to play. This will probably be the kind of music that you also enjoy listening to.

Another thing to consider is whether you'd like to play music alone or as part of a group. If you want to play alone, you might like to play the piano. This would not be a great choice if you'd like to play in a marching band! A trumpet or a trombone would be a better choice for that. If you'd like to play in a small group, you might choose the violin or the cello. String instruments like these are often played together in groups of two to four musicians. If you're imagining playing in a rock band, the guitar or the drums are popular choices. If you imagine yourself playing in a huge orchestra, you have lots of choices. You could play anything from the flute, to the saxophone, to the piano or the drums.

One other thing to consider is whether you would also like to sing as well. Some instruments are great for this, while others are not so good. It would be nearly impossible to sing while playing the trumpet! If you want to sing as well, consider learning the piano or the guitar. Just remember that you will have to work hard on your singing skills as well as your playing skills.

Getting Your Gear

Now you have chosen your instrument, you need to buy it. If it is expensive, you might like to borrow it instead. You might know a friend or relative who plays an instrument. You can ask to borrow an instrument for a little while to try it out. That way, you can make sure it is the right choice before spending lots of money. Some schools or libraries will lend students instruments. Or you can look in your local paper or online for a secondhand instrument.

Getting Ready to Learn

After you have your instrument, you should then create a learning plan. This might involve private lessons with a music teacher or going to music classes. Some people choose to learn on their own. You can use books, movies, web sites, or you can even watch videos online.

To learn quickly, your plan may include a variety of learning methods. Make sure that you attend every lesson or study your books regularly. Also, be sure to practice what you have learned as this is the best way to develop your new skill.

Making Music

Once you have learned enough to play a song, you should start playing for people. Many people get nervous when they first start performing. You might find that you make more mistakes than usual. Don't let this get you down. Remember that you will learn to calm and control your nerves the more you practice. It is often a good idea to start with your family or friends. Or you might play for your music class. Once you become confident, you can then play for larger groups of people.

Keep Going

To become a good musician, you have to keep playing. Keep learning as much as you can and practice often. Challenge yourself to learn more difficult songs as well. As you learn more, you will become better and better. Some people even become good enough to play music as a career.

1. Read this sentence from the passage.

   Playing a musical instrument is a popular pastime for all age ranges.

   What does the word <u>pastime</u> mean?
   - Ⓐ Choice
   - Ⓑ Career
   - Ⓒ Sport
   - Ⓓ Hobby

2. According to the passage, what should you do first?
   - Ⓐ Check to see if your school will lend you an instrument
   - Ⓑ Decide what instrument you would like to play
   - Ⓒ Create a plan for learning to play an instrument
   - Ⓓ Look in your local newspaper for an instrument

3. Under which heading is information provided about deciding what type of instrument to learn to play? Circle the correct answer.

   Making a Choice   Getting Your Gear

   Getting Ready to Learn   Making Music   Keep Going

4 Read this sentence from the passage.

> **Keep learning as much as you can and practice often.**

Which word means the opposite of <u>often</u>?

- Ⓐ Never
- Ⓑ Rarely
- Ⓒ More
- Ⓓ Regularly

5 The author provides the most information in the section "Making a Choice." Explain why you think this is such an important step. Give at least **two** reasons in your answer.

_____

_____

_____

_____

_____

6 The web below lists ways that people can learn to play a musical instrument on their own.

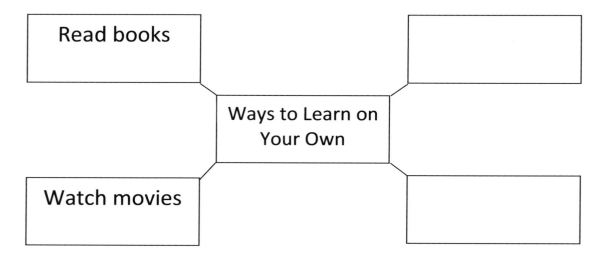

Which of these best complete the web? Write your answers in the web.

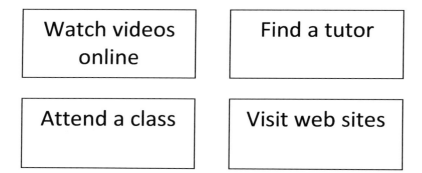

7 What is the main purpose of the passage?

Ⓐ To give readers guidance and advice

Ⓑ To entertain readers with a story

Ⓒ To teach people how to play a musical instrument

Ⓓ To compare different musical instruments

8   Read this sentence from the section "Making Music."

   It is a good idea to start with your family or friends.

   Why does the author most likely suggest starting with your family or friends?

   Ⓐ   So your friends will want to learn to play as well

   Ⓑ   So your family will see that you are trying hard

   Ⓒ   So you feel more comfortable playing

   Ⓓ   So you can have people join in

9   Which sentence from "Making Music" best supports your answer to Question 8?

   Ⓐ   *Many people get nervous when they first start performing.*

   Ⓑ   *You might find that you make more mistakes than usual.*

   Ⓒ   *Remember that you will learn to calm and control your nerves the more you practice.*

   Ⓓ   *Or you might play for your music class.*

10   Why does the author use bullet points in the passage?

   Ⓐ   To highlight the main points

   Ⓑ   To list a set of ideas

   Ⓒ   To show steps to follow in order

   Ⓓ   To describe items that are needed

11 Complete the web below by listing **three** ways you could save money when getting a musical instrument.

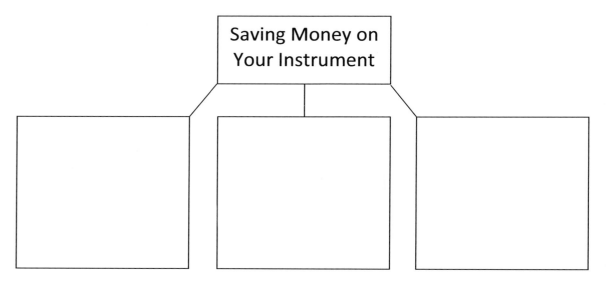

12 The photograph of the girl at the end of the passage is probably included to suggest which of the following?

Ⓐ   How much time and effort it takes to become good at playing

Ⓑ   How it is best to choose an instrument you can play on your own

Ⓒ   How enjoyable and rewarding playing an instrument is

Ⓓ   How it can be difficult to play for an audience at first

13 Complete the graphic organizer below by listing **two** instruments that would be suitable for each purpose.

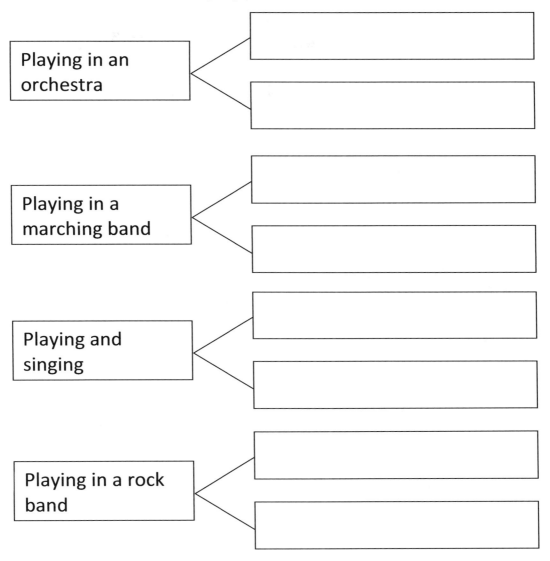

14 If you had to choose a musical instrument to learn to play, which type would you choose? Explain what you considered when making your choice. Use details from the passage in your answer.

END OF SET 11

IAR Practice

Set 12

Short Literary Text

Instructions

This set has one passage for you to read. The passage is followed by questions.

Read each question carefully. For each multiple-choice question, fill in the circle for the correct answer. For other types of questions, follow the instructions given. Some of the questions require a written answer. Write your answer on the lines provided.

Trying Too Hard

Robert was determined to do well in his exams. He devoted all of his spare time to study. He had always wanted to be a lawyer when he grew up. He wanted to go to a good college and enjoy a successful career. Unfortunately, this meant that he was almost always serious. Even though he was young, he was unable to relax and enjoy himself most of the time. His friends often got frustrated that he didn't want to spend much time with them.

Robert had an important exam the following day. He had spent almost an entire week preparing for it. He had managed to get little sleep and was very tired.

He even spent the night before the exam revising and had barely managed any sleep at all. However, he thought that he was ready for the exam. He was confident that he had worked harder than anyone else and was sure to get a perfect grade.

After Robert ate his breakfast, he started to feel a little ill. He was tired and unable to focus. He also had a small headache and found it very difficult to concentrate. He still refused to believe that he could ever fail the exam. Robert arrived at the school hall and took his seat beside his friends. He noticed how relaxed and happy they looked compared to him.

"They are just underprepared," he thought to himself as he began the exam.

Despite his best efforts, Robert struggled. The numbers seemed to swim in front of him. After twenty minutes, he felt very hot and uncomfortable. He then slumped in his chair, and one of his friends called for help. The school doctor suggested that he was exhausted and would be unable to complete the exam.

He spent the lunch break in the nurse's office. He looked out the window and watched his friends. They smiled and joked and seemed to have not a care in the world. Robert decided that from then on, he wouldn't take it quite so seriously. He would study enough, but never too much.

1 What does the word <u>frustrated</u> mean in the sentence below?

His friends often got frustrated that he didn't want to spend much time with them.

- Ⓐ   Worried
- Ⓑ   Annoyed
- Ⓒ   Confused
- Ⓓ   Amused

2 What does the word <u>underprepared</u> mean in the sentence below?

"They are just underprepared," he thought to himself as he began the exam.

- Ⓐ   The most prepared
- Ⓑ   More prepared
- Ⓒ   Not prepared enough
- Ⓓ   Too prepared

3 Think about the genre of "Trying Too Hard." What is the main feature the passage shares with a fable?

- Ⓐ   It features mythical creatures.
- Ⓑ   It involves forces of nature.
- Ⓒ   It has a moral lesson.
- Ⓓ   It is set in the past.

4 Describe **two** important details about Robert's character that are introduced in the first paragraph.

1: _____

_____

2: _____

_____

5 Complete the diagram by listing **four** details the author includes to show that Robert is not well on the day of the exam.

Robert is unwell on the day of the exam.

6 Which sentence best explains why Robert feels ill during the exam?

- Ⓐ Robert had an important exam the following day.
- Ⓑ He had spent almost an entire week preparing for it.
- Ⓒ He even spent the night before the exam revising and had barely managed any sleep at all.
- Ⓓ He was confident that he had worked harder than anyone else and was sure to get a perfect grade.

7 What happens right after Robert slumps in his chair?

- Ⓐ He keeps working on the exam.
- Ⓑ The nurse comes to see him.
- Ⓒ He starts to feel sick.
- Ⓓ His friend calls for help.

8 How does the photograph in the passage suggest that Robert is studying too hard? Explain your answer.

_____

_____

_____

_____

_____

9 Complete the diagram below by describing what Robert expects to happen and what actually happens.

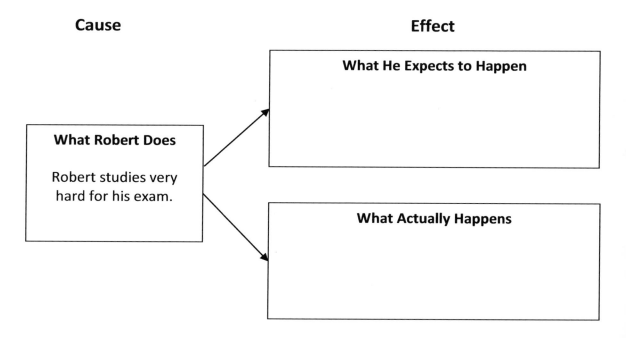

10 Irony occurs when someone's actions have an effect that is the opposite of what was intended. Use your answer to Question 9 to explain why the outcome of the exam is ironic.

_____

_____

_____

_____

_____

11 Which of these describes the main lesson that Robert learns in the passage?

- Ⓐ It is important to have a balanced life.
- Ⓑ It is better to have fun than to do well.
- Ⓒ You should never give up on your goals.
- Ⓓ You can achieve anything if you believe in yourself.

12 Which sentence from the passage best summarizes the lesson you selected in Question 11?

- Ⓐ *Robert was determined to do well in his exams.*
- Ⓑ *He still refused to believe that he could ever fail the exam.*
- Ⓒ *They smiled and joked and seemed to have not a care in the world.*
- Ⓓ *He would study enough, but never too much.*

13 How would the ending of the passage most likely be different if it was told from Robert's point of view?

- Ⓐ The reader would have a better understanding of Robert's feelings about what happened.
- Ⓑ The reader would realize that Robert is probably not really going to change.
- Ⓒ The reader would worry more about whether or not Robert will be allowed to retake the exam.
- Ⓓ The reader would not feel sorry for Robert since what happened was his own fault.

14 At the end of the passage, Robert decides that he shouldn't take things too seriously. Do you think this is a good decision? Explain why or why not.

END OF SET 12

IAR Practice

Set 13

Long Informational Text

Instructions

This set has one passage for you to read. The passage is followed by questions.

Read each question carefully. For each multiple-choice question, fill in the circle for the correct answer. For other types of questions, follow the instructions given. Some of the questions require a written answer. Write your answer on the lines provided.

The Super Bowl

The Super Bowl is the deciding game of the National Football League (NFL). It decides who wins the championship trophy each season. It was first played in the winter of 1967 to find the champion of the 1966 season. Since that time, it has become a major national occasion loved by football fans everywhere. It is a major honor to win the Super Bowl for both teams and their supporters.

At the time it was created, there were two American football leagues. These were the NFL and the AFL, or American Football League. The winners of each league would play against each other to determine which team was the overall champion.

When the two leagues merged, the game was retained. It has since become a game where the top national teams play each other for the main championship. The Green Bay Packers won the first two Super Bowls played in 1967 and 1968. They were considered to be the best team at the time. Many people thought they would continue to win for years to come. This changed in 1969 when the New York Jets won Super Bowl III. This was the last Super Bowl that included teams from separate NFL and AFL leagues.

The game has grown steadily in popularity since this time. It is played annually on a Sunday. The timing of the game has changed since 1970. While it used to be played in early January, it is now played on the first Sunday in February. The Super Bowl game has become a major part of America's culture. It has even been declared a national holiday across the nation.

The Super Bowl has emerged as the most watched television event in America. Super Bowl XLV was played in 2011 and drew a national audience of more than 110 million viewers. The Super Bowl is also one of the most watched sporting events throughout the world. Only the UEFA Champions League trophy in soccer is viewed by a higher global audience.

The Pittsburgh Steelers have won a total of six Super Bowls. They stand alone as the most successful team in the contest's history. The Dallas Cowboys and the San Francisco 49ers have each won the trophy five times. The Pittsburgh Steelers had a chance to win a seventh title in the 2011 Super Bowl. However, they were defeated by the Green Bay Packers. It was the fourth win for the Green Bay Packers.

Sports and Trophies

Trophies are an important part of major sporting leagues. They become a symbol of what every team hopes to achieve and act as a lasting symbol of the winning team's achievements. They often have a long history that makes them even more special.

The Vince Lombardi Trophy

The team that wins the Super Bowl receives the Vince Lombardi Trophy. It is named after the coach of the Green Bay Packers who won the first two Super Bowl games. It was designed by the vice president of Tiffany & Co. in 1966 and the trophies have been made by the company ever since.

It was first presented to the Green Bay Packers in 1967, though it was simply known as the championship trophy at that time. Its name was changed in 1970 after Vince Lombardi passed away. Unlike some other trophies, a new Vince Lombardi trophy is made each year and the winning team keeps that trophy forever.

The Larry O'Brien Championship Trophy

The Larry O'Brien Championship Trophy is awarded to the winning team of the National Basketball Association (NBA) finals each year. The name of the winning team and the year is engraved on the trophy, and given to the winning team to keep. The trophy is named after Larry O'Brien, who was the NBA commissioner from 1975 to 1984.

The trophy is made by Tiffany & Co. each year. It is made from silver alloys and coated in 24 karat gold. The golden color of the trophy is striking and distinguishes it from other trophies. However, despite its striking appearance, it is not as well known as many other sporting trophies.

The Stanley Cup

The Stanley Cup is the most appreciated ice hockey trophy in the world. It is awarded every year to the winner of the National Hockey League (NHL) championships.

Unlike most other sports, a new Stanley Cup is not made each year. Instead, the winning team keeps the trophy until new champions are crowned the next year. This ability to take possession of the trophy for a short time makes players appreciate the award even more. Each winning team also has the names of players, coaches, and other team staff engraved on the trophy. This is considered a great honor by all.

The Stanley Cup is the oldest professional sports trophy in North America. It was donated by the Governor General of Canada, Lord Stanley of Preston, in 1892.

1. Read this sentence from the passage.

   When the two leagues merged, the game was retained.

   Which word means about the same as <u>retained</u>?

   Ⓐ Changed

   Ⓑ Kept

   Ⓒ Improved

   Ⓓ Removed

2. According to the passage, how has the Super Bowl changed since it was introduced?

   Ⓐ It is watched by less people.

   Ⓑ It is played between more teams.

   Ⓒ It is played in a different month.

   Ⓓ It is held on a Saturday.

3. How is the third paragraph mainly organized?

   Ⓐ A problem is described and then a solution is given.

   Ⓑ Events are described in the order they occurred.

   Ⓒ Two teams are compared and contrasted.

   Ⓓ Facts are given to support an argument.

4 Determine whether each sentence in paragraph 1 is a fact or an opinion. Write F or O on each line to show your choice.

___ The Super Bowl is the deciding game of the National Football League (NFL).

___ It decides who wins the championship trophy each season.

___ It was first played in the winter of 1967 to find the champion of the 1966 season.

___ Since that time, it has become a major national occasion loved by football fans everywhere.

___ It is a major honor to win the Super Bowl for both teams and their supporters.

5 According to the passage, which team has won the most Super Bowls?

Ⓐ   Green Bay Packers

Ⓑ   Pittsburgh Steelers

Ⓒ   Dallas Cowboys

Ⓓ   New York Jets

6 Which inference can best be made based on the information in the passage?

Ⓐ   Vince Lombardi was a respected coach.

Ⓑ   Vince Lombardi was replaced after the Green Bay Packers were defeated in 1969.

Ⓒ   Vince Lombardi still coaches the Green Bay Packers today.

Ⓓ   Vince Lombardi was a football player before he became a coach.

7 Which meaning of the word drew is used in the sentence below?

> **Super Bowl XLV was played in 2011 and drew a national audience of more than 110 million viewers.**

- Ⓐ Attracted
- Ⓑ Sketched
- Ⓒ Dragged
- Ⓓ Tied

8 Which statement made in paragraph 1 is best supported by the paragraph below? Explain your answer.

> **The Super Bowl has emerged as the most watched television event in America. Super Bowl XLV was played in 2011 and drew a national audience of more than 110 million viewers. The Super Bowl is also one of the most watched sporting events throughout the world. Only the UEFA Champions League trophy in soccer is viewed by a higher global audience.**

_____

_____

_____

_____

_____

9 Choose **two** sentences from the paragraph below that support the idea that the Super Bowl is a major occasion in the United States. Circle the **two** sentences below.

> The game has grown steadily in popularity since this time. It is played annually on a Sunday. The timing of the game has changed since 1970. While it used to be played in early January, it is now played on the first Sunday in February. The Super Bowl game has become a major part of America's culture. It has even been declared a national holiday across the nation.

10 Based on your answer to Question 9, explain why you chose the two sentences.

_____

_____

_____

_____

_____

_____

11 In the sentence below, which word could best be used in place of appreciate?

> **This ability to take possession of the trophy for a short time makes players appreciate the award even more.**

Ⓐ Notice

Ⓑ Demand

Ⓒ Ignore

Ⓓ Value

12 What makes the Stanley Cup special? In your answer, explain how it differs from the Vince Lombardi Trophy and the Larry O'Brien Championship Trophy.

_____

_____

_____

_____

_____

_____

13 How does the last paragraph of "The Stanley Cup" help show the importance of the trophy?

- Ⓐ It shows that ice hockey has been played for a long time.
- Ⓑ It shows that ice hockey is a national sport.
- Ⓒ It shows the long history of the trophy.
- Ⓓ It shows that the trophy is most important to Canadians.

14 Describe **two** facts given about the Larry O'Brien Championship Trophy.

1: _____

_____

2: _____

_____

15 Describe **two** opinions given about the Larry O'Brien Championship Trophy.

1: _____

_____

2: _____

_____

16 The history of sports can play a major role in making them special today. Explain how the information in the passage supports this idea.

END OF SET 13

IAR Practice

Set 14

Paired Informational Passages

Instructions

This set has two short passages for you to read. Read each passage and answer the questions that follow it.

For each multiple-choice question, fill in the circle for the correct answer. For other types of questions, follow the instructions given. Some of the questions require a written answer. Write your answer on the lines provided.

After reading both passages, you will use information from both passages to answer a question. Write your answer on the lines provided.

Writing a Short Story
By Kevin Baker

Writing a short story is a popular and satisfying hobby for a lot of people. It is also an excellent way to express creative thoughts. Writing a good story is not easy, but it is certainly worth the effort. Here are the steps to take to write a good story.

Step 1

Every story starts with an idea. Start by thinking about the things that you enjoy. These activities are excellent subjects to base your stories on. Other ideas can come from thinking about subjects that you'd like to know more about.

Step 2

Once you have an idea, you can then decide who your main characters are going to be. Consider having both a hero and a villain in your story. This will help to keep your readers interested. A hero is also known as a protagonist, while a villain is known as an antagonist. You'll also need to think of the best location for your story to take place.

Step 3

Before you start writing, you need to plan your story. Most writers plan their stories by creating an outline. An outline is like an overview of the story. It should describe the main events that occur. Your story should have a beginning, a middle, and an end. This will help anyone who reads the story to follow its events.

Step 4

Now that you have your outline, it is time to start writing. Follow your outline and write your story. At this point, your story does not have to be perfect. You will go back and improve it later.

Step 5

The story you have written is your first draft. The next step is to read through it and revise it. Here are some questions to help you decide what might need to be changed:

- Are the events that happen clear?
- Is the story interesting?
- Have I described the characters well?
- Can I use better descriptions to make it more exciting?
- Have I left out any important points?
- Is the start of the story good enough to get the reader interested?
- Would the ending leave the reader feeling satisfied?

Keep working on your story until it is the best you can make it.

Step 6

Once the story is complete, read it in full to ensure that it is well-written and easy to follow. Make sure that all your sentences flow well and are easy to understand. You should also check for any spelling or grammar mistakes.

Step 7

It is now time to get some feedback on your story. Have others read your story so that they can make suggestions for improvements. Think about the advice that people tell you. You do not have to take all the advice given, but you should think about it.

Step 8

Revise your story again based on the feedback you have been given. You should also read through it again to make sure all your sentences are written correctly and to ensure that there are no spelling or grammar errors.

You should now have a well-written, polished, and entertaining story.

1   Read this sentence from the passage.

> **You should now have a well-written, polished, and entertaining story.**

What does the word <u>polished</u> show about the story?

Ⓐ   It is enjoyable to read.

Ⓑ   It is smooth and free from errors.

Ⓒ   It has been well-planned.

Ⓓ   It has a suitable ending.

2   Based on your answer to Question 1, choose the **two** steps that will most ensure that the story is polished. Circle the steps you have chosen. Then explain why you chose those steps.

Step 1   Step 2   Step 3   Step 4

Step 5   Step 6   Step 7   Step 8

_____

_____

_____

_____

_____

3   Read this sentence from the passage.

> **It is also an excellent way to express creative thoughts.**

Which meaning of the word <u>express</u> is used in the sentence?

- Ⓐ   To send something quickly
- Ⓑ   To put into words
- Ⓒ   Plain or clear
- Ⓓ   Direct or fast

4   Which detail about the author would best suggest that the advice in the passage can be trusted?

- Ⓐ   He has kept a diary of his thoughts for many years.
- Ⓑ   He has a college degree.
- Ⓒ   His favorite hobby is reading.
- Ⓓ   He has successfully published many short stories.

5   What is the main purpose of the passage?

- Ⓐ   To teach readers how to do something
- Ⓑ   To encourage people to read more
- Ⓒ   To explain the purpose of writing
- Ⓓ   To compare different types of hobbies

6 Why does the author use bullet points in the passage?

    Ⓐ   To highlight the main points

    Ⓑ   To list a set of ideas

    Ⓒ   To show steps to follow in order

    Ⓓ   To describe items that are needed

7 In which step is the first draft of the story written? Circle the correct step.

    Step 1   Step 2   Step 3   Step 4

    Step 5   Step 6   Step 7   Step 8

8 Explain what the terms <u>protagonist</u> and <u>antagonist</u> mean. Explain why you think having both in the story would help keep the reader interested.

_____

_____

_____

_____

_____

9 According to the passage, what should you do first when writing a story?

- Ⓐ Decide who the main character is going to be
- Ⓑ Write an outline of the story
- Ⓒ Discuss your story idea with other people
- Ⓓ Think of an idea for the story

10 The author states that "writing a good story is not easy." How does the information in the passage support this statement? Use details from the passage in your answer.

_____

_____

_____

_____

_____

_____

The River Bank Creative Writing Group

Creative writing is a great way of expressing yourself. The problem is that many people never try to write. Many people believe that they do not have the ability. At the River Bank Creative Writing Group, we aim to unleash your creativity.

We are based in Brooklyn, New York. We started our community organization in the fall of 2001. In the years since then, we have brought creative writing into the lives of many local residents. It does not matter whether you wish to write creatively as a hobby or as a way of making money. We have experienced and skilled staff to help you achieve success. We start by teaching the very basics of creative writing. Then we develop a program that is unique to your skills and goals. This can focus on writing short stories, poetry, plays, or anything else that interests you.

So what exactly do we offer? Well, our creative workshops are known for their quality. Our teachers include experienced professional writers and editors. They will guide you and help you get started. They will also offer feedback on your writing to help you improve. We also have guest speakers who attend once a week and share their own advice and experience. These are usually published authors who have achieved success in their fields. Our guest list is varied and includes successful poets, short story writers, and novelists. Their practical experience is the key to unlocking your creative talents.

We have achieved some great results at the River Bank Creative Writing Group. In 2005, one of our earliest students had her first novel published. She has since gone on to enjoy two further publications and is known worldwide. In 2009, another of our writers had his first poetry collection published. Thousands of our other writers have emerged from our classes as skilled creative writers.

Our classes can benefit you regardless of your goals. If you wish to unlock your creative skill for an exciting pastime, then we can help you. If you dream of being a published author, then we can help you make that happen. It has never been easier to unlock your creativity. If you have an interest in creative writing, then contact us today. We are waiting to hear from you and ready to help you on your journey!

11 In the sentence below, what does the word <u>unleash</u> mean?

> **At the River Bank Creative Writing Group, we aim to unleash your creativity.**

- Ⓐ Take control of
- Ⓑ Train and shape
- Ⓒ Set free
- Ⓓ Benefit from

12 What is the main purpose of the fourth paragraph?
- Ⓐ To encourage people to take writing seriously
- Ⓑ To show the success of the writing group
- Ⓒ To describe different types of writing styles
- Ⓓ To suggest that getting published is easy

13 Describe **two** details given in the fourth paragraph that support your answer to Question 12.

1: _____

_____

2: _____

_____

14 What does the picture at the end of the passage most likely symbolize?

- Ⓐ How long the writing group has existed for
- Ⓑ How much of an achievement writing a book could be
- Ⓒ How the teachers at the group are very experienced
- Ⓓ How the writing group offers a range of services

15 From the information in the passage, the reader can conclude that the writing group –

- Ⓐ is mainly for young writers
- Ⓑ offers the services for free
- Ⓒ is suited to all types of writers
- Ⓓ considers publishing writers' works

16 The passage was probably written mainly to –

- Ⓐ encourage people to attend the writing group's classes
- Ⓑ highlight the benefits of creative writing
- Ⓒ describe the history of the creative writing group
- Ⓓ convince successful writers to be guest speakers

17 Complete the chart below by listing **three** ways the River Bank Creative Writing Group helps people develop their writing skills.

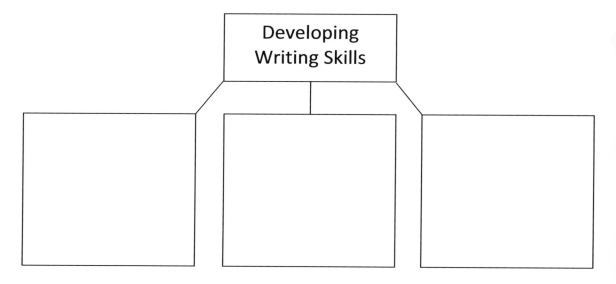

18 Read these sentences from the passage.

> **If you wish to unlock your creative skill for an exciting pastime, then we can help you. If you dream of being a published author, then we can help you make that happen.**

Why does the author most likely include these sentences?

Ⓐ To warn the reader that the workshops may be difficult

Ⓑ To excite the reader about what may be possible

Ⓒ To suggest that the reader should have a clear goal

Ⓓ To describe the successes of past students

19 Which word best describes the tone of the passage?

   Ⓐ   Comforting

   Ⓑ   Straightforward

   Ⓒ   Encouraging

   Ⓓ   Modest

20 Select the **two** sentences from paragraph 2 that best support the idea that the River Bank Creative Writing Group tailors programs to suit each individual. Tick **two** boxes below to show your choices.

   ☐   *We are based in Brooklyn, New York.*

   ☐   *We started our community organization in the fall of 2001.*

   ☐   *In the years since then, we have brought creative writing into the lives of many local residents.*

   ☐   *It does not matter whether you wish to write creatively as a hobby or as a way of making money.*

   ☐   *We have experienced and skilled staff to help you achieve success.*

   ☐   *We start by teaching the very basics of creative writing.*

   ☐   *Then we develop a program that is unique to your skills and goals.*

   ☐   *This can focus on writing short stories, poetry, plays, or anything else that interests you.*

21 Describe how being a good writer involves getting other people to help you. In your answer, describe **two** ways other people can help you develop good writing skills. Use details from both passages in your answer.

END OF SET 14

ANSWER KEY

Illinois Learning Standards

The state of Illinois has adopted the Illinois Learning Standards. Student learning throughout the year is based on these standards, and all the questions on the state tests assess these standards. Just like the real IAR tests, the questions in this book test whether students have the knowledge and skills described in the Illinois Learning Standards. The English Language Arts standards assessed include both reading and writing standards.

Reading Standards

The majority of the questions assess reading standards. These standards are divided into two areas: Reading Standards for Literature and Reading Standards for Informational Text. The answer key on the following pages lists the main standard assessed by each question.

Writing Standards

Writing standards are also assessed on the IAR tests. The writing tasks on the test assess a reading standard as well as one of the writing standards below.

- Write opinion pieces on topics or texts, supporting a point of view with reasons and information.
- Write informative/explanatory texts to examine a topic and convey ideas and information clearly.
- Write narratives to develop real or imagined experiences or events using effective technique, descriptive details, and clear event sequences.

As well as covering the major standards listed above, these questions also cover other more general writing and language standards.

Scoring Questions

The answer key gives guidance on how to score technology-enhanced, constructed-response, essay, and narrative writing questions. Use the criteria listed as a guide to scoring these questions, and as a guide for giving the student advice on how to improve an answer.

IAR Practice, Set 1, Literary Texts with Writing Task

Question	Answer	Reading Standard for Literature
1	creepy ghostly scary	Determine the meaning of words and phrases as they are used in a text, including figurative language such as metaphors and similes.
2	6th, 7th, and 10th	Compare and contrast two or more characters, settings, or events in a story or drama, drawing on specific details in the text.
3	B	Quote accurately from a text when explaining what the text says explicitly and when drawing inferences from the text.
4	See Below	Compare and contrast two or more characters, settings, or events in a story or drama, drawing on specific details in the text.
5	B	Quote accurately from a text when explaining what the text says explicitly and when drawing inferences from the text.
6	A	Determine the meaning of words and phrases as they are used in a text, including figurative language such as metaphors and similes.
7	B	Determine a theme of a story, drama, or poem from details in the text, including how characters in a story or drama respond to challenges or how the speaker in a poem reflects upon a topic; summarize the text.
8	See Below	Explain how a series of chapters, scenes, or stanzas fits together to provide the overall structure of a particular story, drama, or poem.
9	D	Describe how a narrator's or speaker's point of view influences how events are described.
10	A	Compare and contrast two or more characters, settings, or events in a story or drama, drawing on specific details in the text.
11	B	Analyze how visual and multimedia elements contribute to the meaning, tone, or aesthetics of a text.
12	See Below	Quote accurately from a text when explaining what the text says explicitly and when drawing inferences from the text.
13	See Below	Describe how a narrator's or speaker's point of view influences how events are described.
14	B	Determine the meaning of words and phrases as they are used in a text, including figurative language such as metaphors and similes.
15	D	Determine the meaning of words and phrases as they are used in a text, including figurative language such as metaphors and similes.
16	B	Compare and contrast two or more characters, settings, or events in a story or drama, drawing on specific details in the text.
17	See Below	Determine a theme of a story, drama, or poem from details in the text, including how characters in a story or drama respond to challenges or how the speaker in a poem reflects upon a topic; summarize the text.
18	B	Determine the meaning of words and phrases as they are used in a text, including figurative language such as metaphors and similes.
19	B	Compare and contrast stories in the same genre (e.g., mysteries and adventure stories) on their approaches to similar themes and topics.
20	See Below	Explain how a series of chapters, scenes, or stanzas fits together to provide the overall structure of a particular story, drama, or poem.
21	C	Compare and contrast two or more characters, settings, or events in a story or drama, drawing on specific details in the text.
22	C	Determine a theme of a story, drama, or poem from details in the text, including how characters in a story or drama respond to challenges or how the speaker in a poem reflects upon a topic; summarize the text.
23	See Below	Quote accurately from a text when explaining what the text says explicitly and when drawing inferences from the text.
24	See Below	Determine a theme of a story, drama, or poem from details in the text, including how characters in a story or drama respond to challenges or how the speaker in a poem reflects upon a topic; summarize the text.
25	See Below	Compare and contrast two or more characters, settings, or events in a story or drama, drawing on specific details in the text.
26	See Below	Compare and contrast stories in the same genre (e.g., mysteries and adventure stories) on their approaches to similar themes and topics.

Q4.
Give a score of 0, 1, or 2 based on how well the answer meets the criteria listed below.
- It should give a reasonable explanation of how Rick feels based on how he edges toward the door.
- The student should describe how he feels scared, nervous, or uncertain.

Q8.
Give a score of 0, 1, or 2 based on how many relevant details are given.
- Any detail from the passage that shows Rick's fear can be accepted.
- The student may describe how he is quiet on the way to the lighthouse, how he tells Simon to go first, how he is not keen to open the door, or how he shouts and runs away when he hears a noise.

Q12.
Give a score of 0, 1, or 2 based on how well the answer meets the criteria listed below.
- The student should circle one of the words and provide an explanation to support the choice.
- Either answer is acceptable as long as the student explains it and supports it with relevant details.
- The student could argue that Simon is cowardly for being afraid or that Simon is brave for facing his fear.

Q13.
Give a score of 0.5 for each correct factual detail or personal opinion given. A sample answer is given below.
- Factual Details: It is two miles from Simon's house. / It is two hundred years old. / It casts a light for miles.
- Simon's Opinions or Feelings: It is haunted. / It is eerie. / It looks like a ghost at night.

Q17.
Give a score of 0, 1, or 2 based on how well the answer meets the criteria listed below.
- It should give a reasonable explanation of why Tara has mixed feelings about the trip.
- The answer should show an understanding that she is excited about the trip, but scared because she has to fly.

Q20.
Give a score of 0, 1, or 2 based on how well the answer meets the criteria listed below.
- It should explain that Tara's father had a similar experience with a fear he had when he was young.
- It may refer to how Tara's father understands how she feels or understands how she can overcome the fear.

Q23.
Give a score of 1 for each correct cause and effect relationship described. A sample answer is given below.
- Tara is afraid of flying. / Tara doesn't want to go on a trip to New Zealand.
- Tara's father was afraid of spiders. / Tara's father did not want to go camping.

Q24.
Give a score of 0, 1, or 2 based on how well the answer meets the criteria listed below.
- The student should give a reasonable explanation of what Tara means by saying that she is going whether her fear likes it or not. The answer should refer to how she has decided not to give in to fear or not to let fear control her.

Q25.
Give a score of 0, 1, or 2 based on how well the answer meets the criteria listed below.
- It should explain that Tara wanting to do the things in New Zealand makes her braver because it motivates her to overcome her fears. The answer may also refer to how she is going to focus on doing the fun things instead of worrying about her fear.

Q26.
Give a total score out of 7 as described below.
- Give a score of 0, 1, 2, 3, or 4 based on how well the answer shows an understanding of the passages, uses relevant details from both passage, and how well the student expresses ideas. The answer should be well-developed, focused, well-organized, have good transitions, and have an introduction and a conclusion.
- Give a score of 0, 1, 2, or 3 based on how well the student uses the conventions of standard English. The answer should be well-written and have few or no errors in spelling, grammar, punctuation, or capitalization.

IAR Practice, Set 2, Informational Texts with Writing Task

Question	Answer	Reading Standard for Informational Text
1	C	Determine the meaning of general academic and domain-specific words and phrases in a text relevant to a grade 5 topic or subject area.
2	See Below	Determine the meaning of general academic and domain-specific words and phrases in a text relevant to a grade 5 topic or subject area.
3	2, 4, 3, 1	Explain the relationships or interactions between two or more individuals, events, ideas, or concepts in a historical, scientific, or technical text based on specific information in the text.
4	Paragraph 4	Compare and contrast the overall structure of events, ideas, concepts, or information in two or more texts.
5	B	Explain how an author uses reasons and evidence to support particular points in a text, identifying which reasons and evidence support which point(s).
6	B	Quote accurately from a text when explaining what the text says explicitly and when drawing inferences from the text.
7	A	Analyze multiple accounts of the same event or topic, noting important similarities and differences in the point of view they represent.
8	See Below	Explain the relationships or interactions between two or more individuals, events, ideas, or concepts in a historical, scientific, or technical text based on specific information in the text.
9	See Below	Determine two or more main ideas of a text and explain how they are supported by key details; summarize the text.
10	See Below	Draw on information from multiple print or digital sources, demonstrating the ability to locate an answer to a question quickly or to solve a problem efficiently.
11	See Below	Analyze multiple accounts of the same event or topic, noting important similarities and differences in the point of view they represent.
12	A	Determine the meaning of general academic and domain-specific words and phrases in a text relevant to a grade 5 topic or subject area.
13	D	Determine the meaning of general academic and domain-specific words and phrases in a text relevant to a grade 5 topic or subject area.
14	B	Draw on information from multiple print or digital sources, demonstrating the ability to locate an answer to a question quickly or to solve a problem efficiently.
15	D	Analyze multiple accounts of the same event or topic, noting important similarities and differences in the point of view they represent.
16	Paragraph 2	Compare and contrast the overall structure of events, ideas, concepts, or information in two or more texts.
17	See Below	Integrate information from several texts on the same topic in order to write or speak about the subject knowledgeably.
18	See Below	Explain how an author uses reasons and evidence to support particular points in a text, identifying which reasons and evidence support which point(s).
19	See Below	Explain the relationships or interactions between two or more individuals, events, ideas, or concepts in a historical, scientific, or technical text based on specific information in the text.
20	D	Determine two or more main ideas of a text and explain how they are supported by key details; summarize the text.
21	B	Explain the relationships or interactions between two or more individuals, events, ideas, or concepts in a historical, scientific, or technical text based on specific information in the text.
22	B	Compare and contrast the overall structure of events, ideas, concepts, or information in two or more texts.
23	B	Quote accurately from a text when explaining what the text says explicitly and when drawing inferences from the text.
24	See Below	Analyze multiple accounts of the same event or topic, noting important similarities and differences in the point of view they represent.
25	See Below	Explain how an author uses reasons and evidence to support particular points in a text, identifying which reasons and evidence support which point(s).
26	See Below	Integrate information from several texts on the same topic in order to write or speak about the subject knowledgeably.

Q2.
Give a score of 0, 1, or 2 based on how well the answer meets the criteria listed below.
- The answer should identify that the prefix *multi* means many or more than one.
- The student should explain how you can tell the meaning by referring to the languages listed.

Q8.
Give a score of 0, 1, or 2 based on how well the answer meets the criteria listed below.
- It should give a reasonable explanation of why the author includes these details.
- The student may infer that the details are included to show Mark's talent, intelligence, or determination.

Q9.
Give a score of 1 for each correct option added to the web.
- The correct answers are computer programmer and web site developer.

Q10.
Give a score of 0, 1, or 2 based on how well the answer meets the criteria listed below.
- The student should identify one reasonable lesson that can be learned from Mark Zuckerberg.
- The answer may refer to how he developed his talent, how he created something he believed in, how he remained true to himself during the process, or how he gives back to others.

Q11.
Give a score of 0, 1, or 2 based on how well the answer meets the criteria listed below.
- It should give a reasonable explanation of how the photograph and caption shows Zuckerberg's personality.
- It may be positive and refer to him as laid-back or humble or negative and refer to him as lazy or unprofessional.

Q17.
Give a score of 0, 1, or 2 based on how well the answer meets the criteria listed below.
- It should show an understanding that the table summarizes Newton's three laws of motion.
- It should explain how the table gives details about one of Newton's main achievements described in the passage.

Q18.
Give a score of 0, 1, or 2 based on how many correct supporting details are given.
- The answer may refer to how his laws of motion became the foundation for the work of others, how his work in mathematics advanced the theories used today, or how he was voted as the greatest physicist of all time.

Q19.
Give a score 1 for each correct field of study and summary listed in the table. A sample answer is given below.
- Mathematics / He developed the use of fractions and equations.
- Religion / He wrote papers with ideas that went against those of the time.

Q24.
Give a score of 0, 1, or 2 based on how well the answer meets the criteria listed below.
- The student should make a valid inference about how Elisha Gray would have felt and provide support for it.
- The inference could be that Gray felt annoyed, angry, disappointed, or jealous.

Q25.
Give a score of 0, 1, or 2 based on how many correct supporting details are given.
- The supporting details may include that 150,000 American homes had telephones by 1886, that the telephone became used worldwide, that the telephone became a normal part of life, or that telephones became necessary.

Q26.
Give a total score out of 7 as described below.
- Give a score of 0, 1, 2, 3, or 4 based on how well the answer uses relevant information from all three passages, synthesizes ideas from the passages, and how well the student expresses ideas. The answer should be well-developed, focused, well-organized, and have a style that is appropriate to the task.
- Give a score of 0, 1, 2, or 3 based on how well the student uses the conventions of standard English. The answer should be well-written and have few or no errors in spelling, grammar, punctuation, or capitalization.

IAR Practice, Set 3, Literary Text with Narrative Writing Task

Question	Answer	Reading Standard for Literature
1	A	Determine the meaning of words and phrases as they are used in a text, including figurative language such as metaphors and similes.
2	See Below	Determine the meaning of words and phrases as they are used in a text, including figurative language such as metaphors and similes.
3	B	Determine a theme of a story, drama, or poem from details in the text, including how characters in a story or drama respond to challenges or how the speaker in a poem reflects upon a topic; summarize the text.
4	See Below	Quote accurately from a text when explaining what the text says explicitly and when drawing inferences from the text.
5	C	Explain how a series of chapters, scenes, or stanzas fits together to provide the overall structure of a particular story, drama, or poem.
6	See Below	Determine a theme of a story, drama, or poem from details in the text, including how characters in a story or drama respond to challenges or how the speaker in a poem reflects upon a topic; summarize the text.
7	A	Determine the meaning of words and phrases as they are used in a text, including figurative language such as metaphors and similes.
8	C	Explain how a series of chapters, scenes, or stanzas fits together to provide the overall structure of a particular story, drama, or poem.
9	D	Describe how a narrator's or speaker's point of view influences how events are described.
10	B	Determine the meaning of words and phrases as they are used in a text, including figurative language such as metaphors and similes.
11	See Below	Determine a theme of a story, drama, or poem from details in the text, including how characters in a story or drama respond to challenges or how the speaker in a poem reflects upon a topic; summarize the text.
12	4th	Determine the meaning of words and phrases as they are used in a text, including figurative language such as metaphors and similes.
13	See Below	Determine the meaning of words and phrases as they are used in a text, including figurative language such as metaphors and similes.
14	See Below	This question assesses the writing standard below. Write narratives to develop real or imagined experiences or events using effective technique, descriptive details, and clear event sequences.

Q2.
Give a score of 0.5 for each word placed in the correct column.
- Synonyms: tiny, small, little, minute
- Antonyms: giant, massive, huge, great

Q4.
Give a score of 1 for each line that includes a reasonable explanation supporting the choice.
- The explanation for each line should describe how it shows the poet's opinion about how hardworking spiders are.
- Possible lines could include: I watch him as he toils, / Forever building come what may. / He builds his home to be the best. / Think how hard he has to toil, / Without a single word or moan.

Q6.
Give a score of 0, 1, or 2 based on how well the answer meets the criteria listed below.
- It should give a reasonable explanation of how stanza 3 has a message about overcoming disappointments.
- The answer should refer to how the spider does not get upset when his web is broken and simply starts again.

Q11.
Give a score of 0, 1, or 2 based on how well the answer meets the criteria listed below.
- It should give a reasonable explanation of what can be learned about hard work and determination.
- The answer may refer to keeping focused, to not complaining, to being determined to achieve a goal, or to working hard for your family or others.

Q13.
Give a score of 0, 1, or 2 based on how well the answer meets the criteria listed below.
- It should explain the meaning of the metaphor and tell what the metaphor shows about the spider's home.
- The answer should describe how the home as a "castle" shows that it is special to the spider, that it is all the spider cares about, or that it is grand or beautiful.

Q14.
Give a total score out of 6 as described below.
- Give a score of 0, 1, 2, or 3 based on the student's narrative writing skill. The narrative should establish a situation, have a clear event sequence, use effective descriptions, use concrete words and phrases and sensory details, and provide a sense of closure.
- Give a score of 0, 1, 2, or 3 based on how well the student uses the conventions of standard English. The answer should be well-written and have few or no errors in spelling, grammar, punctuation, or capitalization.

IAR Practice, Set 4, Short Informational Text

Question	Answer	Reading Standard for Informational Text
1	A	Determine the meaning of general academic and domain-specific words and phrases in a text relevant to a grade 5 topic or subject area.
2	help, assistance	Determine the meaning of general academic and domain-specific words and phrases in a text relevant to a grade 5 topic or subject area.
3	D	Analyze multiple accounts of the same event or topic, noting important similarities and differences in the point of view they represent.
4	C	Determine two or more main ideas of a text and explain how they are supported by key details; summarize the text.
5	D	Determine two or more main ideas of a text and explain how they are supported by key details; summarize the text.
6	See Below	Explain how an author uses reasons and evidence to support particular points in a text, identifying which reasons and evidence support which point(s).
7	C	Quote accurately from a text when explaining what the text says explicitly and when drawing inferences from the text.
8	See Below	Quote accurately from a text when explaining what the text says explicitly and when drawing inferences from the text.
9	B	Explain the relationships or interactions between two or more individuals, events, ideas, or concepts in a historical, scientific, or technical text based on specific information in the text.
10	1st, 2nd, 4th, and 6th	Draw on information from multiple print or digital sources, demonstrating the ability to locate an answer to a question quickly or to solve a problem efficiently.
11	See Below	Determine two or more main ideas of a text and explain how they are supported by key details; summarize the text.
12	She makes class fun. She explains things clearly.	Determine two or more main ideas of a text and explain how they are supported by key details; summarize the text.
13	C	Compare and contrast the overall structure of events, ideas, concepts, or information in two or more texts.
14	See Below	Quote accurately from a text when explaining what the text says explicitly and when drawing inferences from the text.

Q6.
Give a score of 0, 1, or 2 based on how many correct supporting details are given.
- The answer may refer to how Miss Hooper made every subject fun and interesting, never made Jacob feel silly for asking a question, or explained things several times if she needed to.

Q8.
Give a score of 0, 1, or 2 based on how well the answer meets the criteria listed below.
- The student should explain how you can tell that Jacob is sad about losing Miss Hooper but understanding.
- The answer may refer to his "mixed feelings," to how he is sad about losing her, to how he is glad she will be able to help others, or to how he says it would be selfish to keep her all through school.

Q11.
Give a score of 0, 1, or 2 based on how well the answer meets the criteria listed below.
- It should explain why starting a new school turned out to be a huge blessing for Jacob.
- It should refer to the influence Miss Hooper had on Jacob and how it has changed how he feels about school.

Q14.
Give a score of 0, 1, 2, or 3 based on how well the answer meets the criteria listed below.
- It should describe one quality that Miss Hooper has that the student thinks is important for a good teacher to have.
- It should provide a reasonable explanation of why that quality is important.

IAR Practice, Set 5, Short Literary Text

Question	Answer	Reading Standard for Literature
1	C	Determine the meaning of words and phrases as they are used in a text, including figurative language such as metaphors and similes.
2	See Below	Analyze how visual and multimedia elements contribute to the meaning, tone, or aesthetics of a text.
3	A	Determine a theme of a story, drama, or poem from details in the text, including how characters in a story or drama respond to challenges or how the speaker in a poem reflects upon a topic; summarize the text.
4	A	Explain how a series of chapters, scenes, or stanzas fits together to provide the overall structure of a particular story, drama, or poem.
5	1st and 5th	Determine the meaning of words and phrases as they are used in a text, including figurative language such as metaphors and similes.
6	C	Explain how a series of chapters, scenes, or stanzas fits together to provide the overall structure of a particular story, drama, or poem.
7	B	Determine the meaning of words and phrases as they are used in a text, including figurative language such as metaphors and similes.
8	B	Quote accurately from a text when explaining what the text says explicitly and when drawing inferences from the text.
9	Stanza 5	Compare and contrast two or more characters, settings, or events in a story or drama, drawing on specific details in the text.
10	See Below	Compare and contrast two or more characters, settings, or events in a story or drama, drawing on specific details in the text.
11	B	Determine the meaning of words and phrases as they are used in a text, including figurative language such as metaphors and similes.
12	See Below	Explain how a series of chapters, scenes, or stanzas fits together to provide the overall structure of a particular story, drama, or poem.
13	See Below	Describe how a narrator's or speaker's point of view influences how events are described.
14	See Below	Determine a theme of a story, drama, or poem from details in the text, including how characters in a story or drama respond to challenges or how the speaker in a poem reflects upon a topic; summarize the text.

Q2.
Give a score of 0, 1, or 2 based on how well the answer meets the criteria listed below.
- It should give a reasonable analysis of how the personification helps readers connect with the poem.
- It may refer to how readers understand the lily, understand the lily's feelings, or feel pleased that the lily feels good.

Q10.
Give a score of 0, 1, or 2 based on how well the answer meets the criteria listed below.
- It should identify that the lily feels upset, needy, or impatient in both stanzas 1 and 5.
- It should identify that the lily wants sunshine in the first stanza and rain in the fifth stanza.

Q12.
Give a score of 0, 1, or 2 based on how well the answer meets the criteria listed below.
- It should describe how the lines describe the lily collecting water when it rains.
- It should explain that the water cannot be collected until the sunshine makes the lily's petals stand upright.

Q13.
Give a score of 1 for each stanza identified that includes a reasonable explanation of what the dialogue tells the reader.
- The student may identify stanzas 3, 7, or 8.
- The explanation for each stanza may describe how the lily feels or why the lily feels that way.

Q14.
Give a score of 0, 1, 2, or 3 based on how well the answer meets the criteria listed below.
- It should explain how the weather affects the lily.
- It should use relevant details from the passage, such as how the lily lifts its head when it is in the sunlight, how it droops when there is no rain, or how the lily is healthy after rainfall.

IAR Practice, Set 6, Long Informational Text

Question	Answer	Reading Standard for Informational Text
1	A	Determine the meaning of general academic and domain-specific words and phrases in a text relevant to a grade 5 topic or subject area.
2	D	Analyze multiple accounts of the same event or topic, noting important similarities and differences in the point of view they represent.
3	See Below	Quote accurately from a text when explaining what the text says explicitly and when drawing inferences from the text.
4	A	Draw on information from multiple print or digital sources, demonstrating the ability to locate an answer to a question quickly or to solve a problem efficiently.
5	See Below	Compare and contrast the overall structure of events, ideas, concepts, or information in two or more texts.
6	famous, well-known	Determine the meaning of general academic and domain-specific words and phrases in a text relevant to a grade 5 topic or subject area.
7	A	Explain how an author uses reasons and evidence to support particular points in a text, identifying which reasons and evidence support which point(s).
8	F, F, F, O	Analyze multiple accounts of the same event or topic, noting important similarities and differences in the point of view they represent.
9	See Below	Explain how an author uses reasons and evidence to support particular points in a text, identifying which reasons and evidence support which point(s).
10	B	Integrate information from several texts on the same topic in order to write or speak about the subject knowledgeably.
11	B	Determine two or more main ideas of a text and explain how they are supported by key details; summarize the text.
12	3, 4, 2	Draw on information from multiple print or digital sources, demonstrating the ability to locate an answer to a question quickly or to solve a problem efficiently.
13	A	Determine the meaning of general academic and domain-specific words and phrases in a text relevant to a grade 5 topic or subject area.
14	See Below	Integrate information from several texts on the same topic in order to write or speak about the subject knowledgeably.

Q3.
Give a score of 1 for each row of the table correctly completed. The correct answers are given below.
- Brazil 5 / Italy 4 / Germany 3

Q5.
Give a score of 0.5 for each sentence correctly matched. The correct answers are given below.
- The 2013 championship... – a fact given to support a claim
- This is much less than for... – a comparison
- However, soccer is a very... – an opinion
- Soccer may become a... – a prediction

Q9.
Give a score of 0, 1, or 2 based on how many correct supporting details are given.
- The details may include that the team has won the English Premier League nineteen times, that the team has won the English Premier League more times than any other team, and that the team has won the European Champions League three times.

Q14.
Give a score of 0, 1, 2, or 3 based on how well the answer meets the criteria listed below.
- It should give a reasonable analysis of how the information about David Beckham shows how talented players have been part of the reason for Manchester United's popularity.
- The student may refer to how Beckham became famous, how he helped the team win, or how he drew huge crowds to games.
- It should use relevant details from the passage.

IAR Practice, Set 7, Paired Literary Passages

Question	Answer	Reading Standard for Literature
1	C	Explain how a series of chapters, scenes, or stanzas fits together to provide the overall structure of a particular story, drama, or poem.
2	See Below	Determine a theme of a story, drama, or poem from details in the text, including how characters in a story or drama respond to challenges or how the speaker in a poem reflects upon a topic; summarize the text.
3	A	Determine the meaning of words and phrases as they are used in a text, including figurative language such as metaphors and similes.
4	C	Quote accurately from a text when explaining what the text says explicitly and when drawing inferences from the text.
5	A	Determine the meaning of words and phrases as they are used in a text, including figurative language such as metaphors and similes.
6	C	Quote accurately from a text when explaining what the text says explicitly and when drawing inferences from the text.
7	See Below	Compare and contrast two or more characters, settings, or events in a story or drama, drawing on specific details in the text.
8	B	Describe how a narrator's or speaker's point of view influences how events are described.
9	B	Determine the meaning of words and phrases as they are used in a text, including figurative language such as metaphors and similes.
10	B	Describe how a narrator's or speaker's point of view influences how events are described.
11	See Below	Compare and contrast two or more characters, settings, or events in a story or drama, drawing on specific details in the text.
12	A	Describe how a narrator's or speaker's point of view influences how events are described.
13	B	Determine the meaning of words and phrases as they are used in a text, including figurative language such as metaphors and similes.
14	C	Compare and contrast two or more characters, settings, or events in a story or drama, drawing on specific details in the text.
15	B	Determine the meaning of words and phrases as they are used in a text, including figurative language such as metaphors and similes.
16	D	Quote accurately from a text when explaining what the text says explicitly and when drawing inferences from the text.
17	special and unforgettable	Determine a theme of a story, drama, or poem from details in the text, including how characters in a story or drama respond to challenges or how the speaker in a poem reflects upon a topic; summarize the text.
18	See Below	Explain how a series of chapters, scenes, or stanzas fits together to provide the overall structure of a particular story, drama, or poem.
19	See Below	Quote accurately from a text when explaining what the text says explicitly and when drawing inferences from the text.
20	See Below	Compare and contrast two or more characters, settings, or events in a story or drama, drawing on specific details in the text.
21	See Below	Determine the meaning of words and phrases as they are used in a text, including figurative language such as metaphors and similes.
22	See Below	Compare and contrast stories in the same genre (e.g., mysteries and adventure stories) on their approaches to similar themes and topics.

Q2.
Give a score of 0, 1, or 2 based on how well the answer meets the criteria listed below.
- The student may circle excitement, surprise, or relief.
- The answer should include an analysis of how you can tell how Casey feels based on paragraph 1.

Q11.
Give a score of 0, 1, or 2 based on how well the answer meets the criteria listed below.
- It should compare how Casey expects the day to be with how it turns out.
- The answer should refer to how Casey worries about being ignored or not being liked, but finds everyone friendly and makes new friends easily.

Q18.
Give a score of 0, 1, or 2 based on how well the answer meets the criteria listed below.
- The student should identify that paragraph 2 contains a flashback.
- It should describe how the flashback tells how Emma first felt when she learned she was going to have a brother.

Q19.
Give a score of 0, 1, or 2 based on how well the answer meets the criteria listed below.
- It should give details that show that Emma is excited about having a baby brother.
- The details may include that she cannot sleep the night before, that she cannot concentrate on anything while waiting to go to the hospital, that she feels like the trip to the hospital takes a long time, or that she can't stop smiling when she sees her brother.

Q20.
Give a score of 0, 1, or 2 based on how many relevant details are given.
- The details may include that she does not smile, that she worries about him crying all the time, that she worries about losing her room, or that she thinks her mother might not come to her dance competitions.

Q21.
Give a score of 1 for each phrase added that creates a sense of calm.
- The phrases could include any of the following: took him in my arms; cradled his tiny little baby body; slowly opened his eyes; gazed up at me; deepest blue; smile softly; slowly closed his eyes; or drifted off to sleep.

Q22.
Give a score of 0, 1, 2, or 3 based on how well the answer meets the criteria listed below.
- It should describe how Casey's and Emma's experiences have a message about not being afraid of change.
- It should identify that Casey and Emma are both worried about things changing at first, but that everything turns out well in the end.

IAR Practice, Set 8, Literary Texts with Writing Task

Question	Answer	Reading Standard for Literature
1	B	Determine the meaning of words and phrases as they are used in a text, including figurative language such as metaphors and similes.
2	A	Determine the meaning of words and phrases as they are used in a text, including figurative language such as metaphors and similes.
3	A	Analyze how visual and multimedia elements contribute to the meaning, tone, or aesthetics of a text.
4	C	Quote accurately from a text when explaining what the text says explicitly and when drawing inferences from the text.
5	A	Compare and contrast stories in the same genre (e.g., mysteries and adventure stories) on their approaches to similar themes and topics.
6	See Below	Compare and contrast two or more characters, settings, or events in a story or drama, drawing on specific details in the text.
7	A	Determine a theme of a story, drama, or poem from details in the text, including how characters in a story or drama respond to challenges or how the speaker in a poem reflects upon a topic; summarize the text.
8	See Below	Explain how a series of chapters, scenes, or stanzas fits together to provide the overall structure of a particular story, drama, or poem.
9	B	Compare and contrast two or more characters, settings, or events in a story or drama, drawing on specific details in the text.
10	See Below	Quote accurately from a text when explaining what the text says explicitly and when drawing inferences from the text.
11	misguided reconsider unable	Determine the meaning of words and phrases as they are used in a text, including figurative language such as metaphors and similes.
12	See Below	Quote accurately from a text when explaining what the text says explicitly and when drawing inferences from the text.
13	See Below	Compare and contrast two or more characters, settings, or events in a story or drama, drawing on specific details in the text.
14	B	Determine the meaning of words and phrases as they are used in a text, including figurative language such as metaphors and similes.
15	B	Determine the meaning of words and phrases as they are used in a text, including figurative language such as metaphors and similes.
16	See Below	Determine a theme of a story, drama, or poem from details in the text, including how characters in a story or drama respond to challenges or how the speaker in a poem reflects upon a topic; summarize the text.
17	B	Determine a theme of a story, drama, or poem from details in the text, including how characters in a story or drama respond to challenges or how the speaker in a poem reflects upon a topic; summarize the text.
18	D	Explain how a series of chapters, scenes, or stanzas fits together to provide the overall structure of a particular story, drama, or poem.
19	See Below	Quote accurately from a text when explaining what the text says explicitly and when drawing inferences from the text.
20	D	Describe how a narrator's or speaker's point of view influences how events are described.
21	See Below	Quote accurately from a text when explaining what the text says explicitly and when drawing inferences from the text.
22	See Below	Determine a theme of a story, drama, or poem from details in the text, including how characters in a story or drama respond to challenges or how the speaker in a poem reflects upon a topic; summarize the text.
23	See Below	Determine a theme of a story, drama, or poem from details in the text, including how characters in a story or drama respond to challenges or how the speaker in a poem reflects upon a topic; summarize the text.
24	See Below	Compare and contrast two or more characters, settings, or events in a story or drama, drawing on specific details in the text.
25	See Below	Compare and contrast stories in the same genre (e.g., mysteries and adventure stories) on their approaches to similar themes and topics.

Q6.
Give a score of 0.5 for each correct reason listed in the table. A sample answer is given below.
- Scott's Reasons: Being an inventor has always been his dream. / He want to improve how things are done.
- Luke's Reasons: He should get a regular income. / He might waste all his talent.

Q8.
Give a score of 1 for each paragraph that includes a reasonable explanation supporting the choice.
- The explanation for each paragraph should describe how it relates to the theme of not giving up on your dreams.

Q10.
Give a score of 0, 1, or 2 based on how many correct supporting details are given.
- The answer may refer to how he keeps going when his inventions fail, how he does not let Luke's concerns stop him, or how he says that he cannot stop.

Q12.
Give a score of 1 for each correct benefit listed in the table. A sample answer is given below.
- Motorcycle helmet: Improved rider vision   New airplane wing: Improved efficiency

Q13.
Give a score of 0, 1, or 2 based on how well the answer meets the criteria listed below.
- It should state a fully-supported opinion of whether or not Luke is a good friend to Scott.
- The student may argue that Luke is a good friend because he supported Scott and tried to help and guide him, or that Luke is not a good friend because he did not believe in Scott and tried to get him to choose a practical career.

Q16.
Give a score of 0, 1, or 2 based on how well the answer meets the criteria listed below.
- It should explain that the main problem that Troy has to overcome is that he is too short.
- It may refer to how Troy overcomes the problem by working harder, by having great ball skills, or by being faster.

Q19.
Give a score of 0, 1, or 2 based on how well the answer meets the criteria listed below.
- It should refer to Troy saying he would be the best player in the world and help the coach out one day.

Q21.
Give a score of 0, 1, or 2 based on how well the answer meets the criteria listed below.
- It should make a valid prediction about how the coach feels about his decision to give Troy a chance.
- The prediction could be that the coach is pleased, proud of his decision, or relieved that he made the decision.

Q22.
Give a score of 0, 1, or 2 based on how well the answer meets the criteria listed below.
- It should clearly explain why Troy's story is inspiring. The answer may refer to the message about not giving up on your dreams, about the value of hard work, or about how people can overcome barriers to achieve their dreams.

Q23.
Give a score of 0, 1, 2, or 3 based on how many correct examples are listed in the diagram. A sample answer is given below.
- He practices his ball skills longer than others. / He is fast and can get around others. / Players underestimate him.

Q24.
Give a score of 0, 1, or 2 based on how many correct supporting details are given.
- The student may refer to how he asks the coach for a chance, how he puts everything into the practice match, how he stays on the court to show his skills instead of taking a break, or how he works hard to develop his skills.

Q25.
Give a total score out of 7 as described below.
- Give a score of 0, 1, 2, 3, or 4 based on how well the answer shows an understanding of the passages, uses relevant details from both passage, and how well the student expresses ideas. The answer should be well-developed, focused, well-organized, have good transitions, and have an introduction and a conclusion.
- Give a score of 0, 1, 2, or 3 based on how well the student uses the conventions of standard English. The answer should be well-written and have few or no errors in spelling, grammar, punctuation, or capitalization.

IAR Practice, Set 9, Informational Texts with Writing Task

Question	Answer	Reading Standard for Informational Text
1	See Below	Determine the meaning of general academic and domain-specific words and phrases in a text relevant to a grade 5 topic or subject area.
2	D	Determine the meaning of general academic and domain-specific words and phrases in a text relevant to a grade 5 topic or subject area.
3	See Below	Draw on information from multiple print or digital sources, demonstrating the ability to locate an answer to a question quickly or to solve a problem efficiently.
4	B	Quote accurately from a text when explaining what the text says explicitly and when drawing inferences from the text.
5	A	Compare and contrast the overall structure of events, ideas, concepts, or information in two or more texts.
6	See Below	Quote accurately from a text when explaining what the text says explicitly and when drawing inferences from the text.
7	See Below	Integrate information from several texts on the same topic in order to write or speak about the subject knowledgeably.
8	B	Determine the meaning of general academic and domain-specific words and phrases in a text relevant to a grade 5 topic or subject area.
9	6	Explain how an author uses reasons and evidence to support particular points in a text, identifying which reasons and evidence support which point(s).
10	See Below	Integrate information from several texts on the same topic in order to write or speak about the subject knowledgeably.
11	B	Compare and contrast the overall structure of events, ideas, concepts, or information in two or more texts.
12	C	Explain the relationships or interactions between two or more individuals, events, ideas, or concepts in a historical, scientific, or technical text based on specific information in the text.
13	See Below	Explain how an author uses reasons and evidence to support particular points in a text, identifying which reasons and evidence support which point(s).
14	See Below	Determine two or more main ideas of a text and explain how they are supported by key details; summarize the text.
15	See Below	Quote accurately from a text when explaining what the text says explicitly and when drawing inferences from the text.
16	B	Determine two or more main ideas of a text and explain how they are supported by key details; summarize the text.
17	A	Compare and contrast the overall structure of events, ideas, concepts, or information in two or more texts.
18	1st, 3rd, 4th, and 5th	Draw on information from multiple print or digital sources, demonstrating the ability to locate an answer to a question quickly or to solve a problem efficiently.
19	D	Compare and contrast the overall structure of events, ideas, concepts, or information in two or more texts.
20	A	Explain the relationships or interactions between two or more individuals, events, ideas, or concepts in a historical, scientific, or technical text based on specific information in the text.
21	D	Draw on information from multiple print or digital sources, demonstrating the ability to locate an answer to a question quickly or to solve a problem efficiently.
22	1, 3, 4, 2	Quote accurately from a text when explaining what the text says explicitly and when drawing inferences from the text.
23	B	Compare and contrast the overall structure of events, ideas, concepts, or information in two or more texts.
24	See Below	Explain the relationships or interactions between two or more individuals, events, ideas, or concepts in a historical, scientific, or technical text based on specific information in the text.
25	See Below	Integrate information from several texts on the same topic in order to write or speak about the subject knowledgeably.

Q1.
Give a score of 1 for each word that is correctly defined.
- The student should give a reasonable definition of each word chosen based on how the word is used in the passage.

Q3.
Give a score of 1 for each correct function listed.
- The functions that should be listed are as follows: protecting vital organs; generating blood cells; and storing minerals.

Q6.
Give a score of 0, 1, or 2 based on how well the answer meets the criteria listed below.
- It should identify a detail from the passage that the student found interesting or surprising.
- It should include a brief explanation of why the student found the detail interesting or surprising.

Q7.
Give a score of 0, 1, or 2 based on how well the answer meets the criteria listed below.
- It should draw a reasonable conclusion about the purpose of the section titled "Three Simple Rules."
- It should explain that the purpose of the section is to describe how people can prevent osteoporosis or how people can maintain healthy bones.

Q10.
Give a score of 0, 1, or 2 based on how well the answer meets the criteria listed below.
- It should explain how the information in the box gives advice on how to ensure that food is not stored for too long after it has been opened.

Q13.
Give a score of 0, 1, or 2 based on how many correct supporting details are given.
- The supporting details could include how food poisoning can make people very ill, how 50 million Americans get food poisoning every year, how there are 125,000 people admitted to hospital, or how there are around 3,000 deaths.

Q14.
Give a score of 0, 1, or 2 based on how well the answer meets the criteria listed below.
- It should explain that food poisoning occurs when the food that people eat contains harmful bacteria.

Q15.
Give a score of 0, 1, or 2 based on how well the answer meets the criteria listed below.
- It should refer to the bacteria from meat coming into contact with foods that are not cooked before being eaten.

Q24.
Give a score of 0, 1, or 2 based on how many correct differences are described.
- The student may describe how sneezes remove particles from the nasal cavity and nose, how sneezes are more powerful than coughs, or how sneezes can remove air at great speeds.

Q25.
Give a total score out of 7 as described below.
- Give a score of 0, 1, 2, 3, or 4 based on how well the answer uses relevant information from all three passages, synthesizes ideas from the passages, and how well the student expresses ideas. The answer should be well-developed, focused, well-organized, and have a style that is appropriate to the task.
- Give a score of 0, 1, 2, or 3 based on how well the student uses the conventions of standard English. The answer should be well-written and have few or no errors in spelling, grammar, punctuation, or capitalization.

IAR Practice, Set 10, Literary Text with Narrative Writing Task

Question	Answer	Reading Standard for Literature
1	B	Determine the meaning of words and phrases as they are used in a text, including figurative language such as metaphors and similes.
2	D	Determine the meaning of words and phrases as they are used in a text, including figurative language such as metaphors and similes.
3	A	Explain how a series of chapters, scenes, or stanzas fits together to provide the overall structure of a particular story, drama, or poem.
4	B	Determine a theme of a story, drama, or poem from details in the text, including how characters in a story or drama respond to challenges or how the speaker in a poem reflects upon a topic; summarize the text.
5	See Below	Determine a theme of a story, drama, or poem from details in the text, including how characters in a story or drama respond to challenges or how the speaker in a poem reflects upon a topic; summarize the text.
6	B	Explain how a series of chapters, scenes, or stanzas fits together to provide the overall structure of a particular story, drama, or poem.
7	A	Quote accurately from a text when explaining what the text says explicitly and when drawing inferences from the text.
8	See Below	Compare and contrast two or more characters, settings, or events in a story or drama, drawing on specific details in the text.
9	C	Quote accurately from a text when explaining what the text says explicitly and when drawing inferences from the text.
10	D	Determine a theme of a story, drama, or poem from details in the text, including how characters in a story or drama respond to challenges or how the speaker in a poem reflects upon a topic; summarize the text.
11	See Below	Compare and contrast two or more characters, settings, or events in a story or drama, drawing on specific details in the text.
12	See Below	Compare and contrast stories in the same genre (e.g., mysteries and adventure stories) on their approaches to similar themes and topics.
13	See Below	Determine a theme of a story, drama, or poem from details in the text, including how characters in a story or drama respond to challenges or how the speaker in a poem reflects upon a topic; summarize the text.
14	See Below	This question assesses the writing standard below. Write narratives to develop real or imagined experiences or events using effective technique, descriptive details, and clear event sequences.

Q5.
Give a score of 0, 1, or 2 based on how well the answer meets the criteria listed below.
- It should give a reasonable summary of how the outcome for the wasps teaches a lesson about being honest.
- The answer should show an understanding that the wasps lied and were caught lying.

Q8.
Give a score of 0, 1, or 2 based on how well the answer meets the criteria listed below.
- It should give a reasonable explanation of how the wasps panicking affects the judge.
- The answer should refer to how the judge realizes that the wasps must not be able to make honey.

Q11.
Give a score of 0.5 for each correct similarity or difference and for each correct effect listed. A sample answer is given below.
- Similarity: The bees and wasps have yellow and black striped bodies. / Nobody can be sure whether it was the bees or the wasps near the tree.
- Difference: Only the bees can make honey. / The wasps panic when they are asked to make honey.

Q12.
Give a score of 0, 1, or 2 based on how well the answer meets the criteria listed below.
- It should give valid reasons that show that the events could not really happen. The reason given should describe how the animals act in ways that only humans act.

Q13.
Give a score of 0, 1, or 2 based on how well the answer meets the criteria listed below.
- It should describe the main problem as being that nobody can tell whether the honey belongs to the wasps or the bees.
- It should clearly explain how the problem is resolved. This should refer to how the judge tells the wasps and bees to make honey, and realizes by how the wasps respond that they are unable to make honey.

Q14.
Give a total score out of 6 as described below.
- Give a score of 0, 1, 2, or 3 based on the student's narrative writing skill. The narrative should establish a situation, have a clear event sequence, use effective descriptions, use concrete words and phrases and sensory details, and provide a sense of closure.
- Give a score of 0, 1, 2, or 3 based on how well the student uses the conventions of standard English. The answer should be well-written and have few or no errors in spelling, grammar, punctuation, or capitalization.

IAR Practice, Set 11, Short Informational Text

Question	Answer	Reading Standard for Informational Text
1	D	Determine the meaning of general academic and domain-specific words and phrases in a text relevant to a grade 5 topic or subject area.
2	B	Explain the relationships or interactions between two or more individuals, events, ideas, or concepts in a historical, scientific, or technical text based on specific information in the text.
3	Making a Choice	Compare and contrast the overall structure of events, ideas, concepts, or information in two or more texts.
4	B	Determine the meaning of general academic and domain-specific words and phrases in a text relevant to a grade 5 topic or subject area.
5	See Below	Explain the relationships or interactions between two or more individuals, events, ideas, or concepts in a historical, scientific, or technical text based on specific information in the text.
6	Watch videos online / Visit web sites	Quote accurately from a text when explaining what the text says explicitly and when drawing inferences from the text.
7	A	Analyze multiple accounts of the same event or topic, noting important similarities and differences in the point of view they represent.
8	C	Explain the relationships or interactions between two or more individuals, events, ideas, or concepts in a historical, scientific, or technical text based on specific information in the text.
9	A	Explain how an author uses reasons and evidence to support particular points in a text, identifying which reasons and evidence support which point(s).
10	B	Compare and contrast the overall structure of events, ideas, concepts, or information in two or more texts.
11	See Below	Determine two or more main ideas of a text and explain how they are supported by key details; summarize the text.
12	C	Draw on information from multiple print or digital sources, demonstrating the ability to locate an answer to a question quickly or to solve a problem efficiently.
13	See Below	Determine two or more main ideas of a text and explain how they are supported by key details; summarize the text.
14	See Below	Draw on information from multiple print or digital sources, demonstrating the ability to locate an answer to a question quickly or to solve a problem efficiently.

Q5.
Give a score of 0, 1, or 2 based on how well the answer meets the criteria listed below.
- It should give at least two plausible reasons that tell why choosing an instrument is such an important step.
- The answer may refer to not wasting money on the wrong instrument, to being sure to choose an instrument that suits how you want to play it, or to choosing an instrument that you will be able to learn.

Q11.
Give a score of 0, 1, 2, or 3 based on how many ways from the passage are listed. A sample answer is given below.
- Borrow it from a friend or relative. / Borrow it from your school. / Buy a secondhand instrument.

Q13.
Give a score of 0.5 for each correct pair of instruments listed. A sample answer is given below.
- Orchestra: flute / saxophone
- Playing and singing: piano / guitar
- Marching band: trumpet / trombone
- Rock band: guitar / drums

Q14.
Give a score of 0, 1, 2, or 3 based on how well the answer meets the criteria listed below.
- It should state which instrument the student would choose to play.
- It should provide a fully-supported explanation of why the student made that choice.
- It should use relevant details from the passage to explain the choice made.

IAR Practice, Set 12, Short Literary Text

Question	Answer	Reading Standard for Literature
1	B	Determine the meaning of words and phrases as they are used in a text, including figurative language such as metaphors and similes.
2	C	Determine the meaning of words and phrases as they are used in a text, including figurative language such as metaphors and similes.
3	C	Compare and contrast stories in the same genre (e.g., mysteries and adventure stories) on their approaches to similar themes and topics.
4	See Below	Explain how a series of chapters, scenes, or stanzas fits together to provide the overall structure of a particular story, drama, or poem.
5	See Below	Quote accurately from a text when explaining what the text says explicitly and when drawing inferences from the text.
6	C	Compare and contrast two or more characters, settings, or events in a story or drama, drawing on specific details in the text.
7	D	Determine a theme of a story, drama, or poem from details in the text, including how characters in a story or drama respond to challenges or how the speaker in a poem reflects upon a topic; summarize the text.
8	See Below	Analyze how visual and multimedia elements contribute to the meaning, tone, or aesthetics of a text.
9	See Below	Compare and contrast two or more characters, settings, or events in a story or drama, drawing on specific details in the text.
10	See Below	Compare and contrast two or more characters, settings, or events in a story or drama, drawing on specific details in the text.
11	A	Determine a theme of a story, drama, or poem from details in the text, including how characters in a story or drama respond to challenges or how the speaker in a poem reflects upon a topic; summarize the text.
12	D	Determine a theme of a story, drama, or poem from details in the text, including how characters in a story or drama respond to challenges or how the speaker in a poem reflects upon a topic; summarize the text.
13	A	Describe how a narrator's or speaker's point of view influences how events are described.
14	See Below	Quote accurately from a text when explaining what the text says explicitly and when drawing inferences from the text.

Q4.
Give a score of 1 for each relevant detail about Robert's character described.
- The student may describe how he is always studying, how he tries very hard at school, how he is determined to do well at school, how he is always serious, or how he hardly ever relaxes or has fun.

Q5.
Give a score of 0.5 for each detail listed that shows Robert is not well. A sample answer is given below.
- He is tired. / He is unable to focus. / He has a headache. / He cannot concentrate.

Q8.
Give a score of 0, 1, or 2 based on how well the answer meets the criteria listed below.
- It should provide a reasonable analysis of how the photograph shows that Robert is studying too hard.
- It may refer to how serious Robert looks, to how he looks like he is studying hard, to how the numbers and equations suggest he is trying to take in too much information, or to how it suggests that he is overwhelmed.

Q9.
Give a score of 1 for each correct effect given. A sample answer is given below.
- What He Expects to Happen: He will do well on the exam.
- What Actually Happens: He cannot complete the exam.

Q10.
Give a score of 0, 1, or 2 based on how well the answer meets the criteria listed below.
- It should provide a reasonable explanation of how the outcome of the exam is ironic.
- The answer should show an understanding that it is ironic that in trying to do very well on the exam, Robert actually made himself do very poorly on it.

Q14.
Give a score of 0, 1, 2, or 3 based on how well the answer meets the criteria listed below.
- It should explain whether the student believes that Robert's decision to be less serious was a good decision.
- It should provide a fully-supported explanation of why or why not.
- It should use relevant details from the passage.

IAR Practice, Set 13, Long Informational Text

Question	Answer	Reading Standard for Informational Text
1	B	Determine the meaning of general academic and domain-specific words and phrases in a text relevant to a grade 5 topic or subject area.
2	C	Draw on information from multiple print or digital sources, demonstrating the ability to locate an answer to a question quickly or to solve a problem efficiently.
3	B	Compare and contrast the overall structure of events, ideas, concepts, or information in two or more texts.
4	F, F, F, O, O	Analyze multiple accounts of the same event or topic, noting important similarities and differences in the point of view they represent.
5	B	Quote accurately from a text when explaining what the text says explicitly and when drawing inferences from the text.
6	A	Explain the relationships or interactions between two or more individuals, events, ideas, or concepts in a historical, scientific, or technical text based on specific information in the text.
7	A	Determine the meaning of general academic and domain-specific words and phrases in a text relevant to a grade 5 topic or subject area.
8	See Below	Explain how an author uses reasons and evidence to support particular points in a text, identifying which reasons and evidence support which point(s).
9	See Below	Explain how an author uses reasons and evidence to support particular points in a text, identifying which reasons and evidence support which point(s).
10	See Below	Determine two or more main ideas of a text and explain how they are supported by key details; summarize the text.
11	D	Determine the meaning of general academic and domain-specific words and phrases in a text relevant to a grade 5 topic or subject area.
12	See Below	Explain the relationships or interactions between two or more individuals, events, ideas, or concepts in a historical, scientific, or technical text based on specific information in the text.
13	C	Compare and contrast the overall structure of events, ideas, concepts, or information in two or more texts.
14	See Below	Quote accurately from a text when explaining what the text says explicitly and when drawing inferences from the text.
15	See Below	Analyze multiple accounts of the same event or topic, noting important similarities and differences in the point of view they represent.
16	See Below	Quote accurately from a text when explaining what the text says explicitly and when drawing inferences from the text.

Q8.
Give a score of 0, 1, or 2 based on how well the answer meets the criteria listed below.
- It should identify that the paragraph supports the statement that the Super Bowl "has become a major national occasion loved by football fans everywhere."
- It should provide a reasonable summary of how the paragraph supports the statement. The answer should refer to how it is watched by over 110 million American viewers and may also refer to how it is watched all over the world.

Q9.
Give a score of 1 for each correct sentence circled. The possible correct sentences are listed below.
- The game has grown steadily in popularity since this time. / It is played annually on a Sunday. / While it used to be played in early January, it is now played on the first Sunday in February. / The Super Bowl game has become a major part of America's culture. / It has even been declared a national holiday across the nation.

Q10.
Give a score of 0, 1, or 2 based on how well the answer meets the criteria listed below.
- It should give a reasonable explanation of how each sentence chosen shows that the Super Bowl is a major occasion.
- The answer could be based on explicit statements, such as the game becoming more popular or being a national holiday. It could also be based on inferences made from the information, such as that it being played on the first Sunday in February shows that it is an American tradition.

Q12.
Give a score of 0, 1, or 2 based on how well the answer meets the criteria listed below.
- It should explain why the Stanley Cup is special and describe how it differs from the other trophies.
- The answer should refer to how a new trophy is not made each year, and may also refer to it being the oldest trophy.

Q14.
Give a score of 0, 1, or 2 based on how many correct facts are given. Any of the facts below could be listed.
- It is awarded to the winning team of the NBA. / The year and winning team is engraved on it. / It is named after Larry O'Brien. / It is made by Tiffany & Co. / It is made from silver alloys. / It is coated in gold.

Q15.
Give a score of 0, 1, or 2 based on how many correct opinion are given. Any of the opinions below could be listed.
- It has a striking golden color. / Its color makes it stand out from other trophies. / It is not as well known as other sporting trophies.

Q16.
Give a score of 0, 1, 2, or 3 based on how well the answer meets the criteria listed below.
- It should describe how the information in the passage shows how the history of a sport makes it special.
- It may refer to the history of the Super Bowl, the history of teams, the history of significant figures like Vince Lombardi, or the history of sporting trophies.

IAR Practice, Set 14, Paired Informational Passages

Question	Answer	Reading Standard for Informational Text
1	B	Determine the meaning of general academic and domain-specific words and phrases in a text relevant to a grade 5 topic or subject area.
2	See Below	Explain the relationships or interactions between two or more individuals, events, ideas, or concepts in a historical, scientific, or technical text based on specific information in the text.
3	B	Determine the meaning of general academic and domain-specific words and phrases in a text relevant to a grade 5 topic or subject area.
4	D	Analyze multiple accounts of the same event or topic, noting important similarities and differences in the point of view they represent.
5	A	Determine two or more main ideas of a text and explain how they are supported by key details; summarize the text.
6	B	Compare and contrast the overall structure of events, ideas, concepts, or information in two or more texts.
7	Step 4	Draw on information from multiple print or digital sources, demonstrating the ability to locate an answer to a question quickly or to solve a problem efficiently.
8	See Below	Quote accurately from a text when explaining what the text says explicitly and when drawing inferences from the text.
9	D	Explain the relationships or interactions between two or more individuals, events, ideas, or concepts in a historical, scientific, or technical text based on specific information in the text.
10	See Below	Determine two or more main ideas of a text and explain how they are supported by key details; summarize the text.
11	C	Determine the meaning of general academic and domain-specific words and phrases in a text relevant to a grade 5 topic or subject area.
12	B	Compare and contrast the overall structure of events, ideas, concepts, or information in two or more texts.
13	See Below	Explain how an author uses reasons and evidence to support particular points in a text, identifying which reasons and evidence support which point(s).
14	B	Draw on information from multiple print or digital sources, demonstrating the ability to locate an answer to a question quickly or to solve a problem efficiently.
15	C	Quote accurately from a text when explaining what the text says explicitly and when drawing inferences from the text.
16	A	Determine two or more main ideas of a text and explain how they are supported by key details; summarize the text.
17	See Below	Quote accurately from a text when explaining what the text says explicitly and when drawing inferences from the text.
18	B	Explain how an author uses reasons and evidence to support particular points in a text, identifying which reasons and evidence support which point(s).
19	C	Analyze multiple accounts of the same event or topic, noting important similarities and differences in the point of view they represent.
20	4th, 7th, or 8th	Explain how an author uses reasons and evidence to support particular points in a text, identifying which reasons and evidence support which point(s).
21	See Below	Integrate information from several texts on the same topic in order to write or speak about the subject knowledgeably.

Q2.
Give a score of 0, 1, or 2 based on how well the answer meets the criteria listed below.
- The student should circle two steps and provide a reasonable description of how those steps would create a polished story. The most likely steps to be circled are 5, 6, or 8.
- The answer must describe how the two steps would create a polished story.

Q8.
Give a score of 0, 1, or 2 based on how well the answer meets the criteria listed below.
- It should identify that the protagonist is the hero of the story and the antagonist is the villain of the story.
- It should give a reasonable explanation of why having both would keep the story interesting, such as by explaining that the reader would want the hero to overcome the villain.

Q10.
Give a score of 0, 1, or 2 based on how well the answer meets the criteria listed below.
- It should identify details that show that writing a good story is not easy.
- The details may include that it takes many steps to write a good story, that many things need to be considered when writing a story, or that a good story needs to be checked and revised.

Q13.
Give a score of 0, 1, or 2 based on how many correct supporting details are given.
- The supporting details given should be those that show the success of the writing group.
- The answer may refer to the student getting her novel published and becoming known worldwide, to the student having a poetry collection published, or to the thousands of skilled creative writers produced.

Q17.
Give a score of 1 for each correct way of developing writing skills listed. A sample answer is given below.
- Teaches the basics of creative writing. / Gives writers feedback. / Has guest speakers give advice.

Q21.
Give a score of 0, 1, 2, or 3 based on how well the answer meets the criteria listed below.
- It should describe how other people can help you become a good writer and give two examples from the passages of how other people can help.
- The answer may refer to getting feedback from others on your writing, getting guidance from successful writers, or having people teach you how to write well.

Made in the USA
Lexington, KY
30 March 2019